WELSH WALKS

DOLGELLAU AND THE CAMBRIAN COAST

by Laurence Main and Morag Perrott

Wilmslow, United Kingdom

First published in 1992 by Sigma Leisure - an imprint of Sigma Press, 1 South Oak Lane, Wilmslow, Cheshire SK9 6AR, England.

British Library Cataloguing in Publication Data
A CIP record of this book is available from the British Library

ISBN: 1-85058-227-0

Printed and bound by
Ashford Press, Hillsons Road, Curdridge, Southampton.

Cover Design: Morag Perrott.

Walks selected and described by Laurence Main.

All artwork, including sketches, maps and hand-written text by Morag Perrott

CONTENTS

THE WALKS

(continued overleaf)

CONTENTS continued

THE WALKS - Location Map

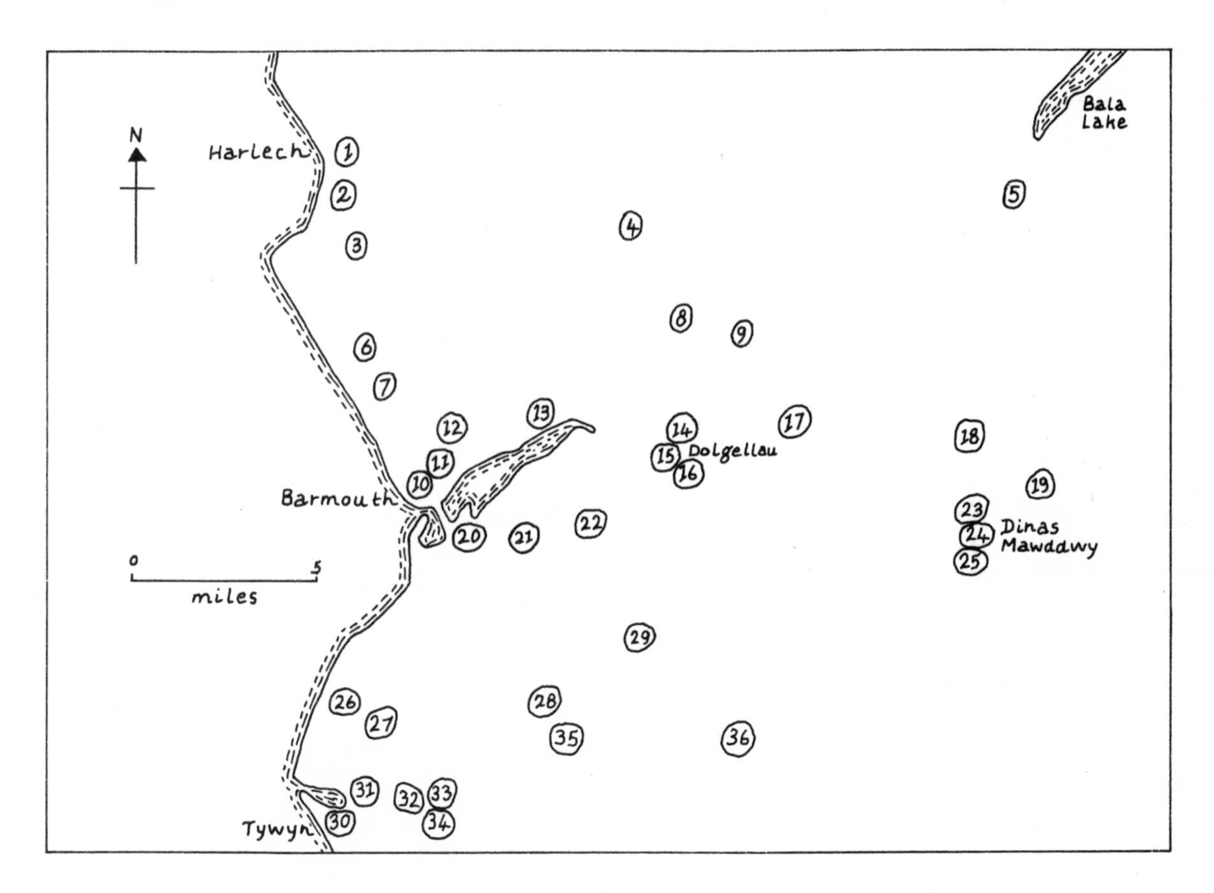

SEA, LAKES AND MOUNTAINS

Dolgellau, the old county town of Meirionnydd is an ideal centre for a walking holiday in the southern part of the Snowdonia National Park. The 2928ft peak of Cadair Idris is well known, while Aran Fawddwy's 2971ft make it the highest summit in Great Britain south of the Snowdon range. The routes up these mountains are well documented as is the traverse of the Rhinogs by the Cambrian Way. This book describes some of the more secret routes which are also less demanding. There is no lack of interest, however, with a variety of paths leading to all sorts of attractions. Woodland paths, forest tracks, fieldpaths, moorland tracks and quiet lanes pass a famous castle, steam trains, ancient monuments, magnificent view-points, a gold mine, slate caverns, ruined abbeys, an authentic site of a corpse candle and a phantom funeral, an aircrash, grave of a Welsh religious heroine and two chapels where her namesake preached in the 1905 revival at the same time as strange earth lights were seen in the sky nearby, nature reserves and scenic lakes which reflect the surrounding mountain slopes. There are also paths which have been made easy to follow by the erection of stiles and waymarks only recently as a result of pressure from the Local Group of the Ramblers' Association.

Altogether there are about 90 miles of walking routes described in the form of short, circular, walks to encourage the inexperienced and experienced walker alike. Some routes can be linked together to form longer walks, as with nos 10, 11 and 12, giving the option of a two, a four or a six mile walk from Barmouth. Many of the walks are located on or near the Cambrian Coast, with its popular resorts, where holidaymakers enjoy the beaches, often without realising that attractive walks are so close. Most routes are accessible by public transport, with British Rail's halts coming into their own and Dolgellau serving as the hub of the Bws Gwynedd network in Meirionnydd. If you do meet a local farmer, he is more than likely to exchange pleasant words with you and to help you with your Welsh. Consideration for the land-owner is expected, of course, while the mountains are also to be respected. Remember the Country Code and dress sensibly, with good footwear, and take the relevant Ordnance Survey Outdoor Leisure map. The route maps in this book are drawn at the generous scale of six inches to one mile (1:10560) to allow relevant details, such as stiles, gates, fences and walls, to be shown. Remember that the countryside is always changing with new fences, for example, liable to be erected. Look out for the new stiles too!

Laurence Main (Footpaths Secretary, Meirionnydd Local Group of the Ramblers' Association).

ROUTE 1

HARLECH

1½ miles

Moderate

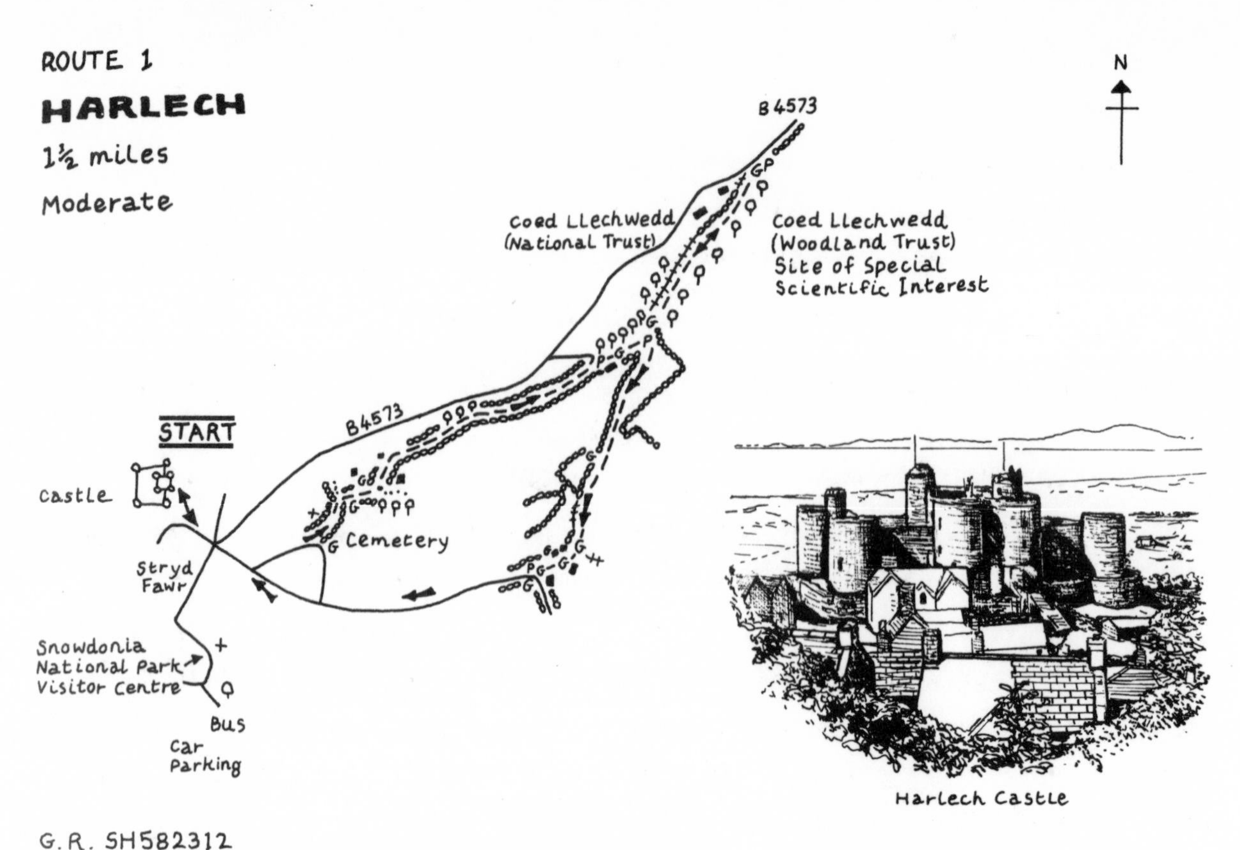

Harlech Castle

G.R. SH582312

O.S Outdoor Leisure map 18 Snowdonia: Harlech & Bala areas

Route 1, **Harlech**

Parking:
There are signposted car parks in Harlech

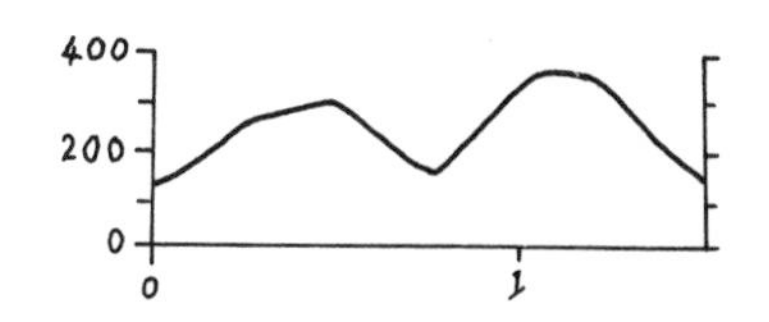

Public Transport:
Harlech has a station on British Rail's Cambrian Coast Line and is served by bus no 38 from Barmouth and Blaenau Ffestiniog

Harlech Castle is an official World Heritage Site. An excellent guide book is available at its entrance. Allow plenty of time to explore the castle then relax with this short, invigorating walk, which will allow you a fine view of it from above. A descending path is followed into Coed Llechwedd. Ash, rowan and sycamore are more common than oak here because the underlying rock is less acidic than beneath most of the surrounding woodlands. The understorey is formed by blackthorn, hazel and hawthorn, Sallow grows in the wetter areas. The range of flowers and ferns includes dogs mercury, ransoms, cuckoo pint, pignut, red campion, wood anemone and opposite-leaved golden saxifrage. The birdlife covers buzzard, heron, pied flycatcher, woodcock, redstart, wood warbler, chiff-chaff, willow warbler, tawny owl and lesser and greater spotted woodpeckers.

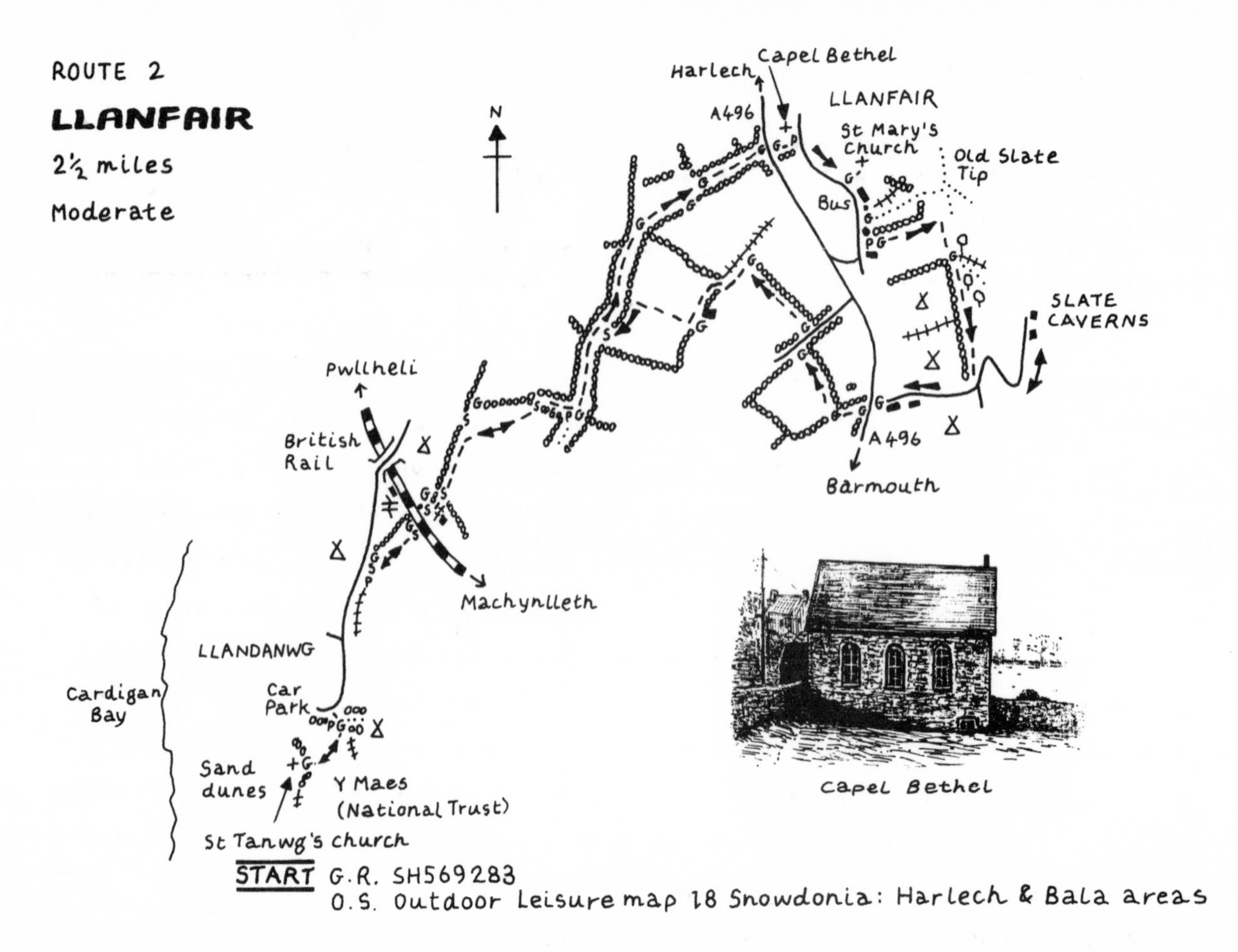

Capel Bethel

Route 2, Llanfair

Parking:
Near the Old Church, Llandanwg
(also near Llanfair's Slate Caverns)

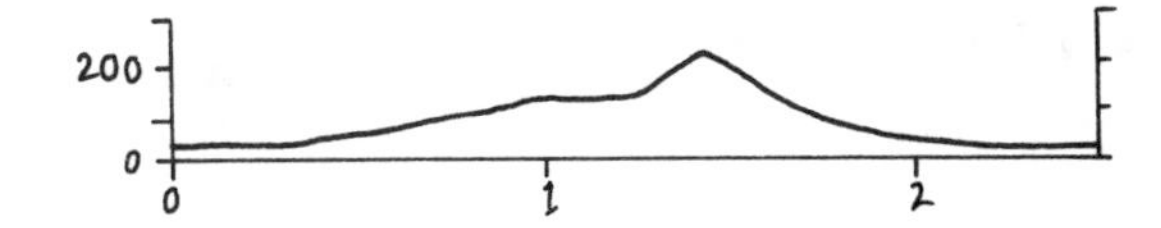

Public Transport:
British Rail has a request halt at Llandanwg on its Cambrian Coast Line (between Machynlleth and Pwllheli). Bus no 38 (Barmouth - Blaenau Ffestiniog via Harlech) stops near St Mary's church, Llanfair.

The climb to the Slate Caverns above Llanfair is well worth the effort. A souvenir guide book is available as are guided tours (n.b. take warm clothing on a hot day - the temperature in the caverns is a constant 50°F). The churches and chapel encountered on this walk are also of interest. St Tanwg's church is swept clear of the encroaching sand for Sunday afternoon services during the holiday season. St Mary's church is dedicated to the Mother of Jesus, who is said to have landed here. She walked towards Hafod-y-Llyn, a lake two miles east of Llanfair, where she bathed. On the way, she knelt to drink from a stream. Marks were left in the rock where she had knelt and a miraculous healing spring arose from its side. Perhaps there is a connection with the strange lights witnessed at 9.15pm on 25th March 1905, near Llanfair's Capel Bethel, during the Mary Jones Revival (and on the Mochras fault - see 'Earth Lights Revelation' by Paul Devereux).

ROUTE 3

LLANBEDR

2½ miles

Moderate

G.R. SH 585269 O.S. Outdoor Leisure map 18
Snowdonia - Harlech & Bala areas

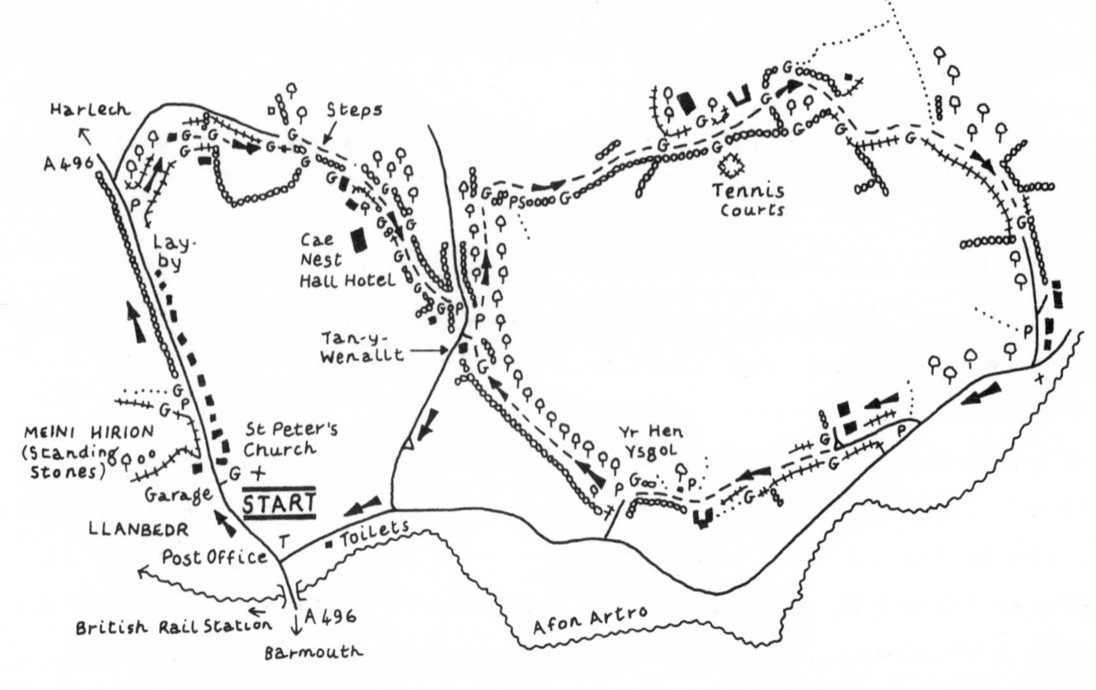

Route 3, Llanbedr

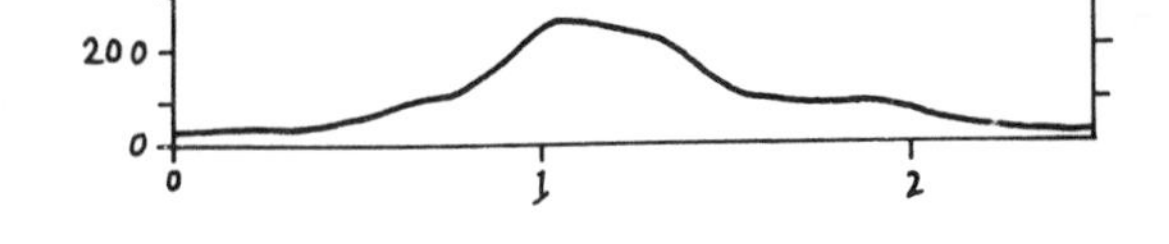

Parking:
There is a lay-by beside the A496 just to the north of Llanbedr (marked on the map).

Public Transport:
Llanbedr has a station on British Rail's Cambrian Coast Line between Machynlleth and Pwllheli. Bus no 38 between Barmouth and Blaenau Ffestiniog stops near Llanbedr Post Office.

Visit St Peter's church, Llanbedr (key available from the doctor's surgery next door), to see a stone carved with a spiral in either the Neolithic or Bronze Age. It came from the Irishmen's huts above Dyffryn Ardudwy and is obviously of great significance. It is unique in Wales and emphasises the importance of this area in prehistory. From the 1850 s to the early 1900 s it was kept between the two standing stones known as Meini Hirion about 200 yards west of the church. One of the stones stands an impressive 10ft high, dwarfing its 6ft 6ins neighbour. With such stones in the vicinity, the dedication to St Peter seems appropriate.

ROUTE 4

MAESGWM

2¾ miles

Moderate

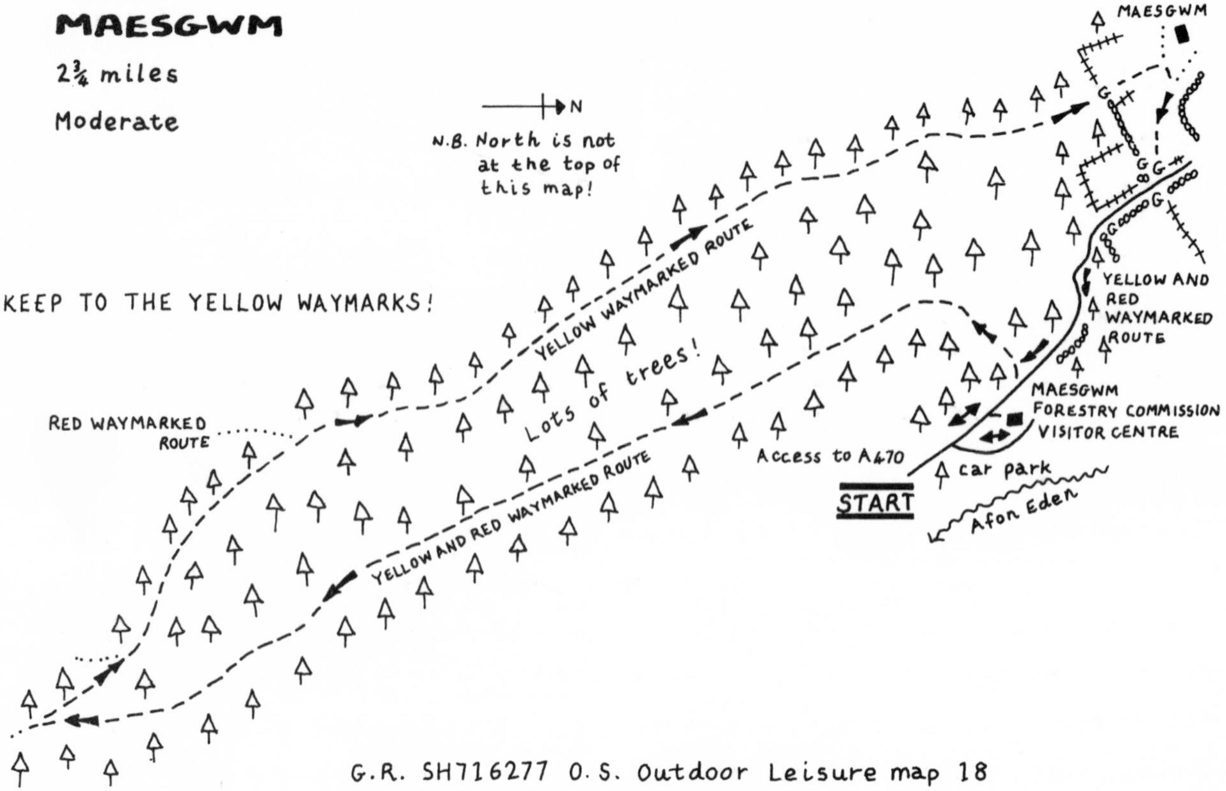

N

N.B. North is not at the top of this map!

KEEP TO THE YELLOW WAYMARKS!

MAESGWM

YELLOW WAYMARKED ROUTE

Lots of trees!

YELLOW AND RED WAYMARKED ROUTE

RED WAYMARKED ROUTE

YELLOW AND RED WAYMARKED ROUTE

G G G G G

MAESGWM FORESTRY COMMISSION VISITOR CENTRE

Access to A470

car park

START

Afon Eden

G.R. SH716277 O.S. Outdoor Leisure map 18
Snowdonia - Harlech & Bala areas.

Route 4, **Maesgwm**

Parking:
There is a car park at the Maesgwm Forestry Commission Visitor Centre.

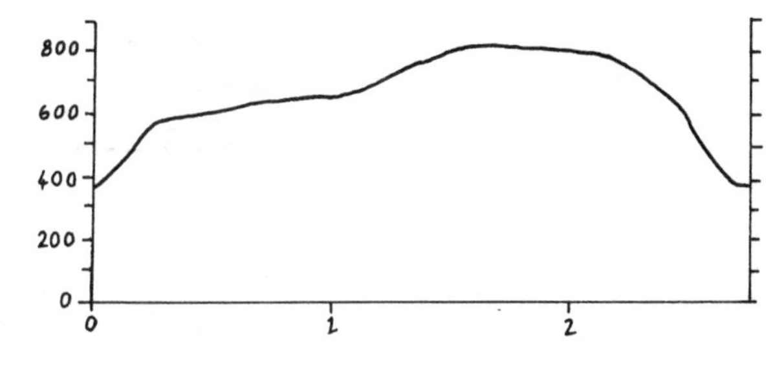

Public Transport:
Bus no 2 (Aberystwyth - Caernarfon via Dolgellau) and bus no 35 (Dolgellau - Blaenau Ffestiniog) pass the access road to the Maesgwm Forestry Commission Visitor Centre where it meets the A470 near Pont Dol-gefeiliau. Ask the driver to set you down here and give vigorous hand signals to be picked up.

Firm forest tracks and good waymarking (follow the yellow route) make this a fairly easy walk. It does climb to provide good views. Most of the trees are either Sitka spruce (used to make paper) or larch (used for fence posts). This is part of the Coed y Brenin (King's Forest). The Maesgwm Visitor Centre is clearly signed from the A470 and is worth a visit (open daily 10 - 5 Easter - September). Refreshments are available and there is a picnic place near the car park.

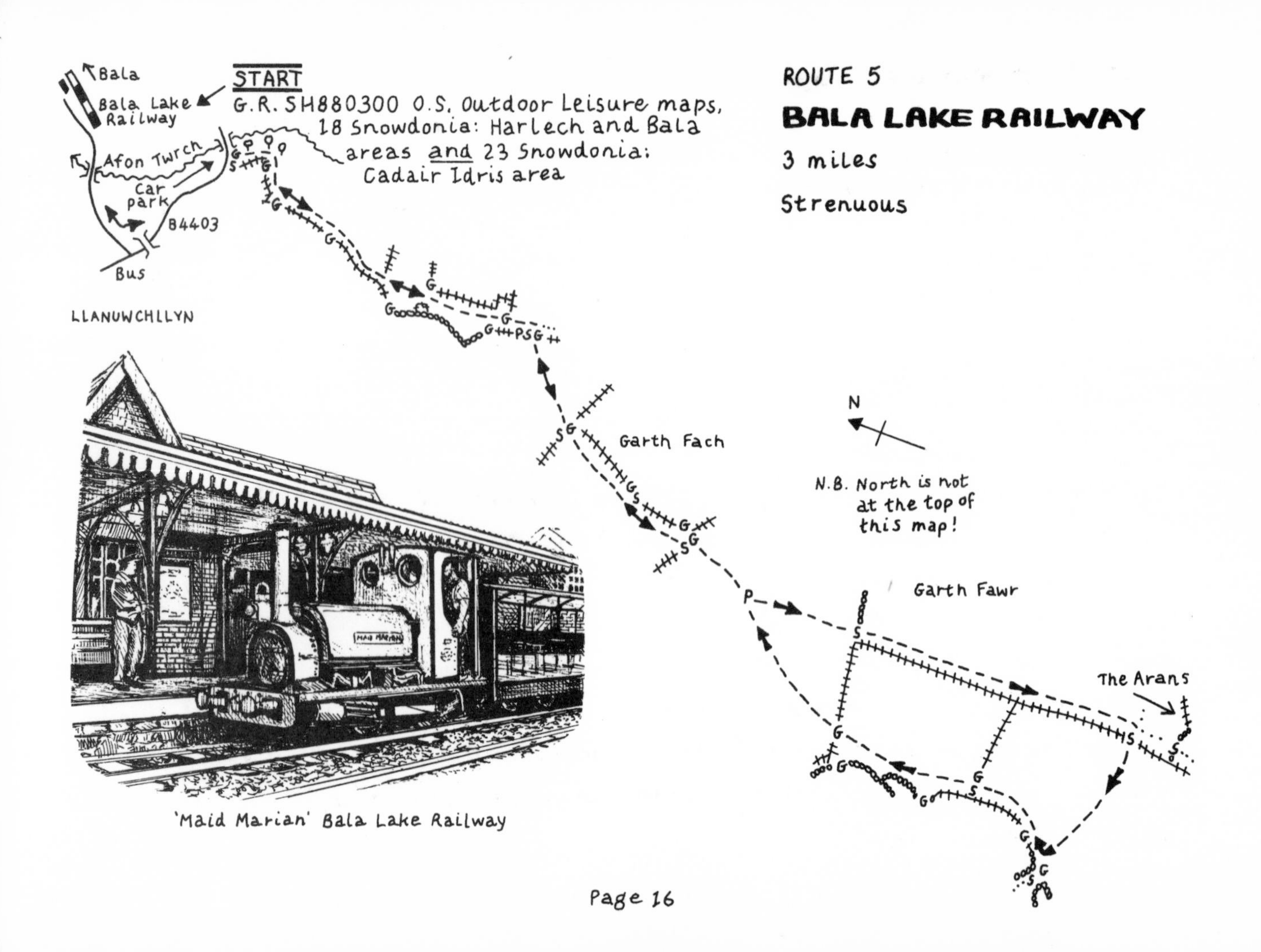

'Maid Marian' Bala Lake Railway

Route 5, Bala Lake Railway

Parking:
Beside the B4403 near the bridge over the Afon Twrch in Llanuwchllyn.

Public Transport:
Seasonal service on the Bala Lake Railway from Bala (tel. 06784 666 for details). Bus no 94 to Llanuwchllyn from Barmouth, Dolgellau, Bala and Wrexham.

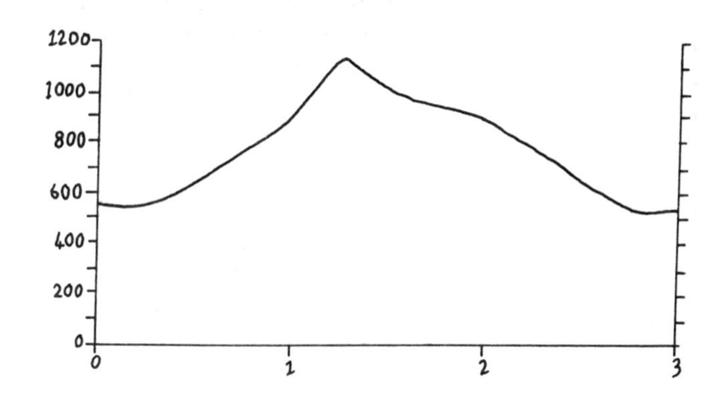

Combine this walk with a trip on the Bala Lake Railway. This 1ft 11½ ins gauge line follows the route of the old Barmouth Junction to Ruabon line past Bala Lake. The trains give excellent views of the lake from its shore, but this walk gives you an overall view of the largest natural lake in Wales from the path which climbs up the Arans. The wild nature of this mountain range is sampled before the return, while Arenig Fawr provides a magnificent backdrop. The paths are waymarked and easy to find. Please maintain good relations with the farmers by not bringing a dog onto this sheep pasture.

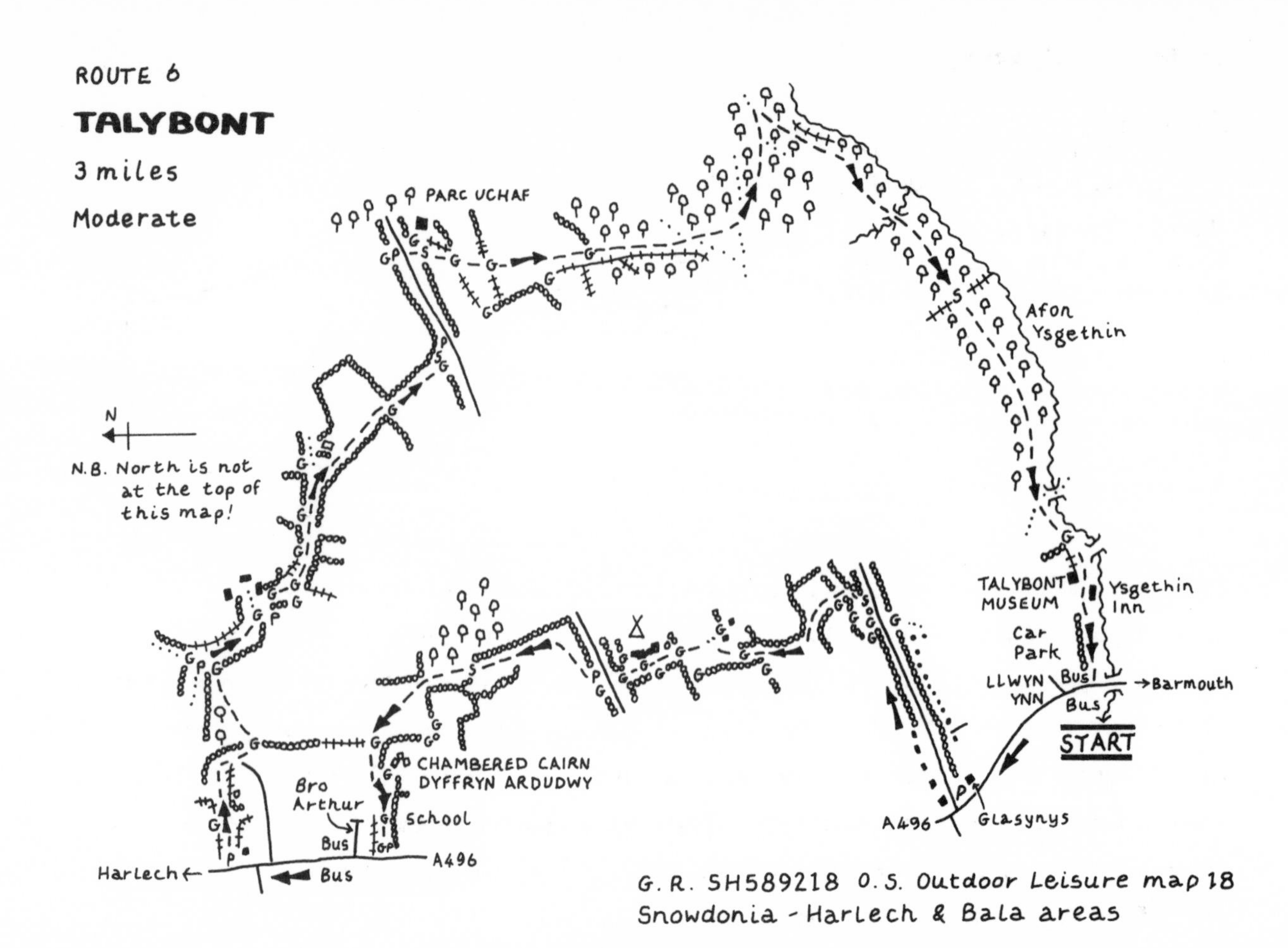

ROUTE 6
TALYBONT
3 miles
Moderate
PARC UCHAF
N
N.B. North is not at the top of this map!
Afon Ysgethin
TALYBONT MUSEUM
Ysgethin Inn
Car Park
LLWYN YNN
Bus
Bus
→Barmouth
START
CHAMBERED CAIRN DYFFRYN ARDUDWY
Bro Arthur
Bus
School
A496
Harlech←
Bus
A496
Glasynys
G.R. SH589218 O.S. Outdoor Leisure map 18
Snowdonia - Harlech & Bala areas

Route 6, Talybont

Parking:
There is a car park near the museum at Talybont.

Public Transport:
Both Talybont and Dyffryn Ardudwy have request halts on British Rail's Cambrian Coast Line (Machynlleth-Pwllheli). Both places are also served by bus no 38 between Barmouth and Blaenau Ffestiniog.

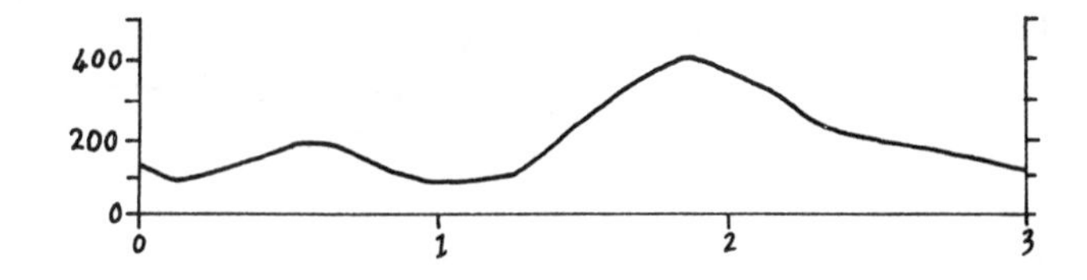

Talybont has an interesting museum showing the old, agricultural, country life. With the Ysgethin Inn nearby, this makes an ideal place to finish a walk. The chambered cairn at Dyffryn Ardudwy is an important Neolithic monument. It is unusual in having two separate megalithic burial chambers. These may or may not have been covered originally. Now they stand on a bed of boulders. Dowsing suggests that a ley runs through them towards Craig y Dinas and Diffwys. The woodland walk above the Afon Ysgethin is delightful.

ROUTE 7

CAPEL EGRYN

2 miles

Moderate

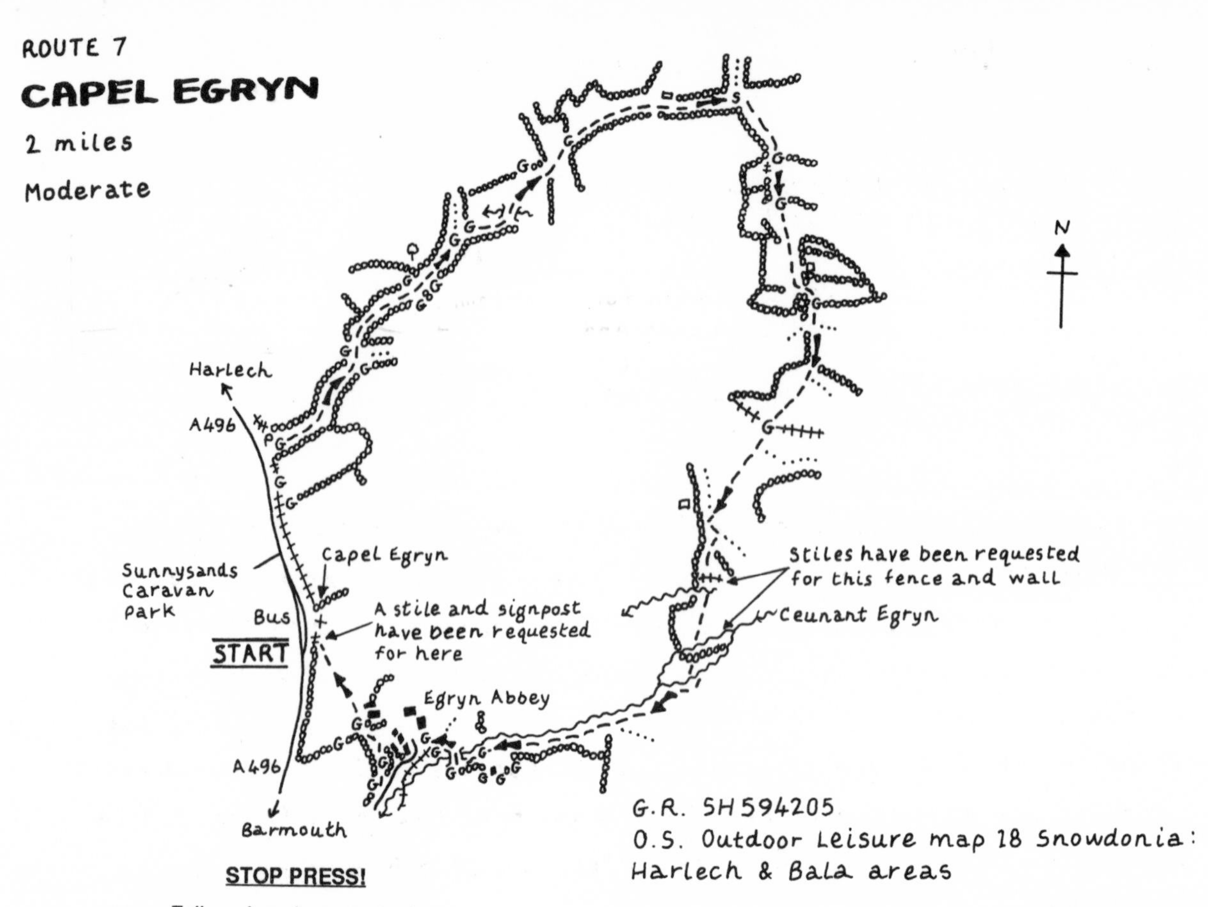

G.R. SH594205

O.S. Outdoor Leisure map 18 Snowdonia: Harlech & Bala areas

STOP PRESS!

Follow signed access track from Egryn Abbey to the A496, then turn right to Capel Egryn.

Route 7, Capel Egryn

<u>Parking</u>:
There is space for parking cars at the start of this walk at Capel Egryn.

<u>Public Transport</u>:
There is a bus stop at Capel Egryn for the no 38 service between Barmouth and Blaenau Ffestiniog via Harlech. Other buses run between Barmouth and Sunnysands caravan park in the summer.

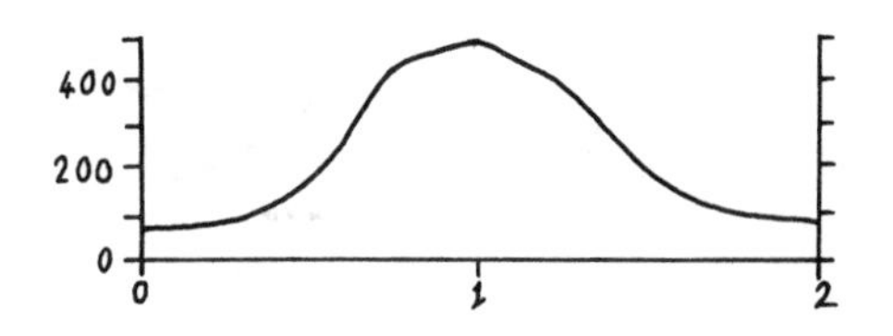

This is a sacred spot associated with the seventh century St Egryn. The Mary Jones revival of 1905 coincided with the appearance of strange lights. Seen as Divine signs by the local populace, these attracted the attention of journalists. The man sent from the London 'Daily Mail' witnessed an intensely brilliant yellow light about 50 feet above Egryn Chapel at about 8.20pm on Saturday 11th February 1905. A 'Daily Mirror' reporter saw an unusually brilliant light here four days later. A full discussion of these is contained in 'Earth Lights Revelation' by Paul Devereux.

ROUTE 8

TY'N-Y-GROES

3 miles

Strenuous

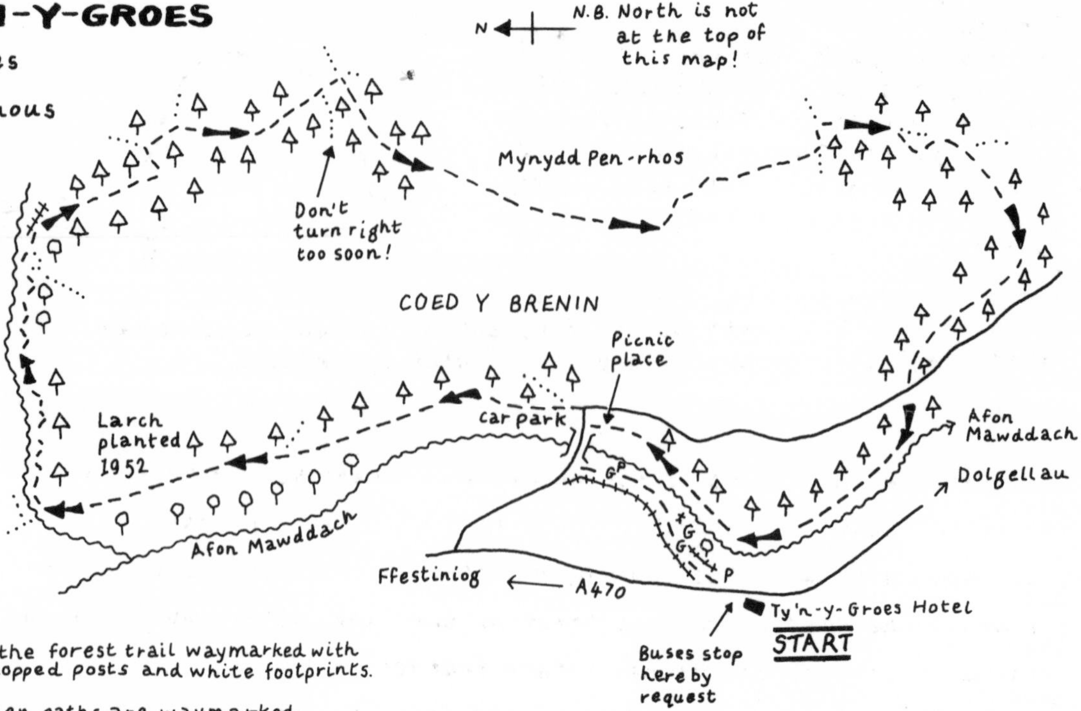

N

N.B. North is not at the top of this map!

Mynydd Pen-rhos

Don't turn right too soon!

COED Y BRENIN

Picnic place

car park

Larch planted 1952

Afon Mawddach

Afon Mawddach

Dolgellau

Ffestiniog

A470

Ty'n-y-Groes Hotel

START

Buses stop here by request

Follow the forest trail waymarked with green-topped posts and white footprints.

N.B. Other paths are waymarked with the white footprints as well.

G.R. SH 728232 O.S. Outdoor Leisure map 23 Snowdonia - Cadair Idris area

Route 8, Ty'n-y-groes

Parking:
Patrons can park near the Ty'n-y-groes Hotel on the A470 north of Dolgellau. There is a large Forestry Commission car park down an access road and across a bridge over the Afon Mawddach.

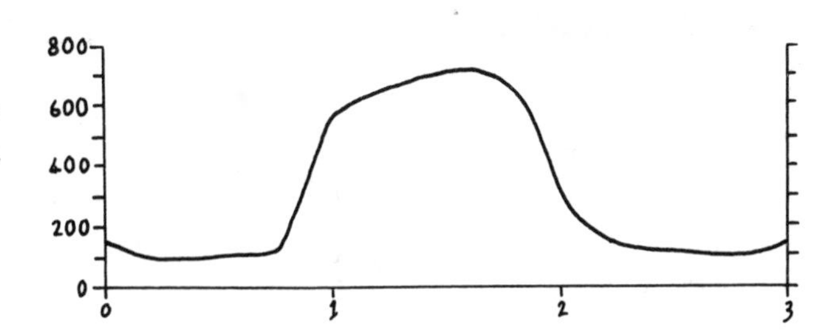

Public Transport:
Buses no 2 (Aberystwyth-Caernarfon) and 35 (Dolgellau-Blaenau Ffestiniog) stop at the Ty'n-y-groes Hotel by request.

This well defined route is set within the Forest Nature Reserve. The steep ascent is through Douglas firs which were planted in 1928. Open ground at the top may provide a view of the fallow deer for which the Coed y Brenin (Forest of the King) is famous. This was originally part of the Nannau estate founded in 1100 by Cadwgan, Prince of Powys. It became part of the Forestry Commission's land in 1922 and was renamed in 1935 to commemorate King George V's Silver Jubilee.

ROUTE 9

LLANFACHRETH

2¾ miles

Moderate

Come in late May to enjoy the bluebells!

G.R. SH754225 O.S. Outdoor Leisure map 23
Snowdonia: Cadair Idris area

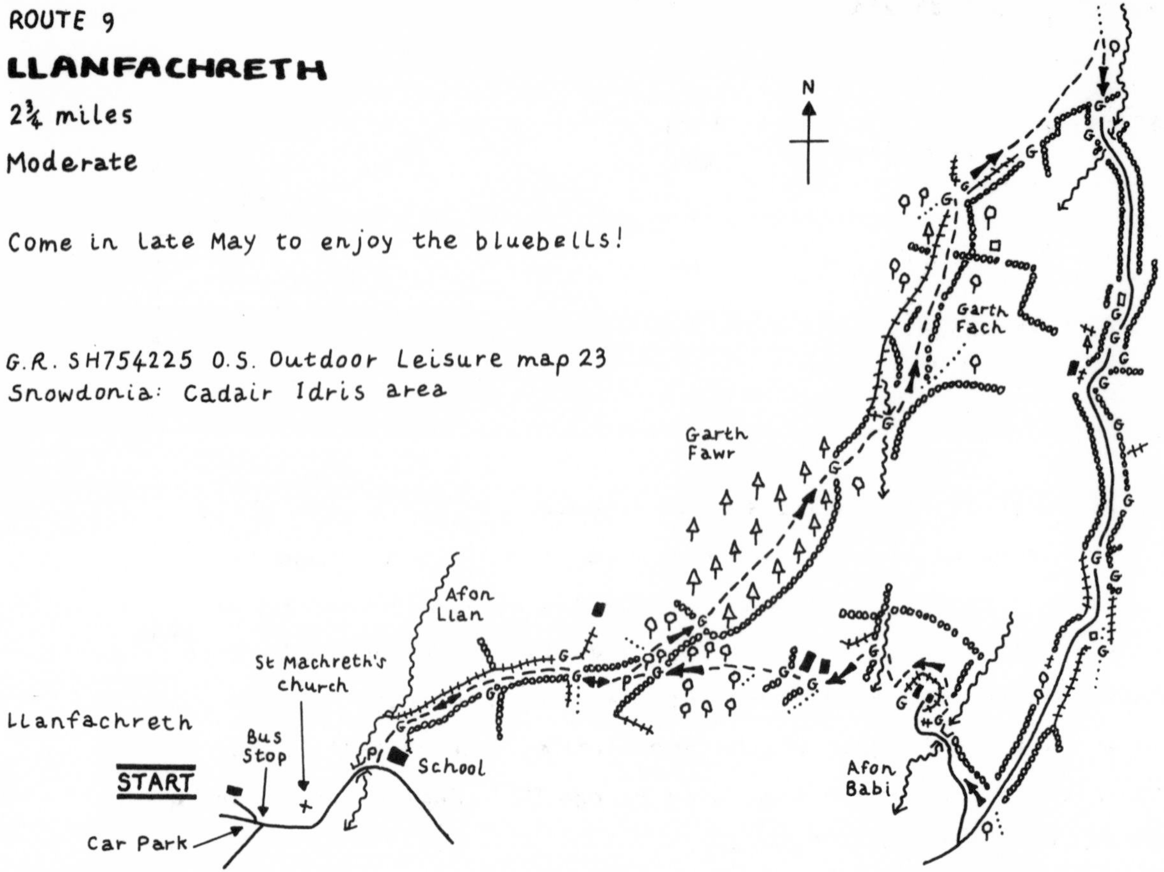

N

Garth Fach

Garth Fawr

Afon Llan

St Machreth's church

Llanfachreth

Bus Stop

START

Car Park

School

Afon Babi

Parking:
Near the war memorial, Llanfachreth

Public Transport:
Bus no 33 from Dolgellau (sometimes continuing as no 27 to Aberangell before returning to Dolgellau). Infrequent.

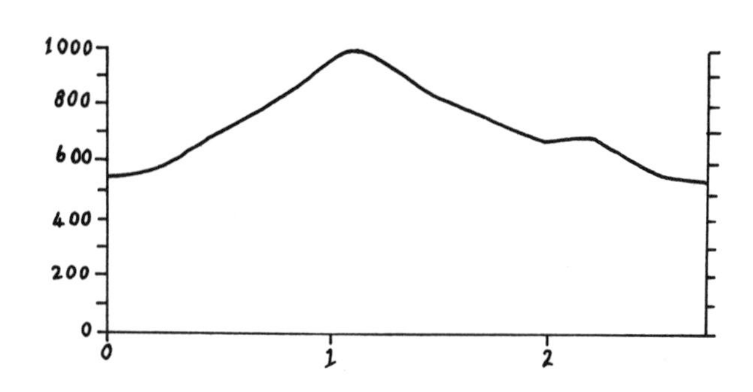

Llanfachreth is high and seemingly remote, yet it is just three miles from Dolgellau. It is named after St Machreth, whose church was rebuilt by the Victorians. Notice the unusual monument to Mrs Anne Nanney, who died in 1729, and also the memorial to Rhys Jones, the eminent Welsh poet who died in 1801. There is also a tablet on the lych-gate which commemorates 'the people's Father and Friend' - none other than King George III! Cadair Idris can be seen to the south on a fine day.

ROUTE 10

BARMOUTH

2¼ miles

Strenuous

G.R. SH 612158 O.S. Outdoor Leisure map 18 Snowdonia - Harlech & Bala areas or map 23 Snowdonia - Cadair Idris area

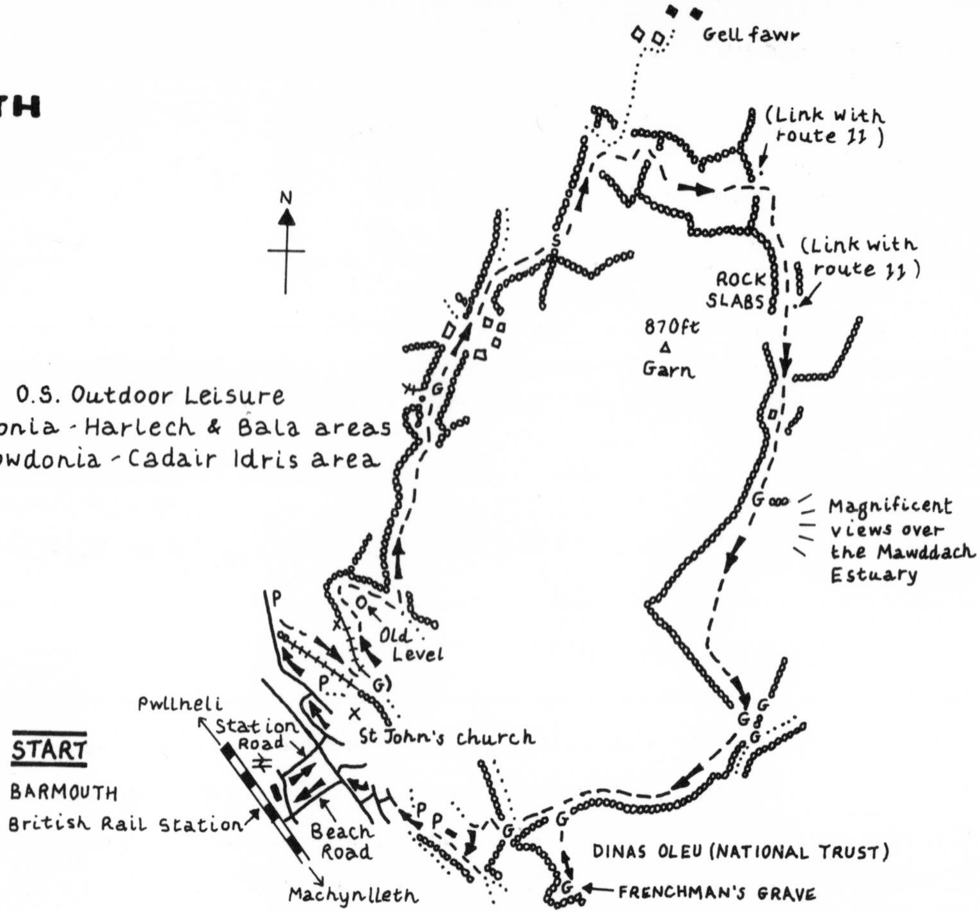

N

Gell fawr

(Link with route 11)

(Link with route 11)

ROCK SLABS

870ft

Garn

Magnificent views over the Mawddach Estuary

Old Level

St John's church

Pwllheli

Station Road

START

BARMOUTH

British Rail Station

Beach Road

Machynlleth

DINAS OLEU (NATIONAL TRUST)

FRENCHMAN'S GRAVE

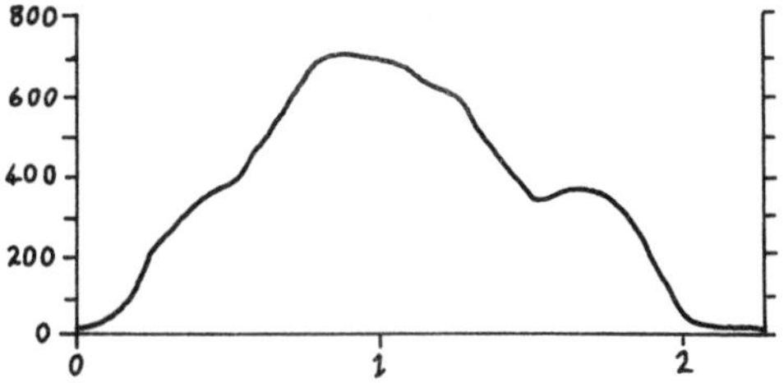

Parking:
There are car parks signposted in Barmouth

Public Transport:
Barmouth is on British Rail's Cambrian Coast Line between Machynlleth and Pwllheli. It can also be reached by bus from Blaenau Ffestiniog via Harlech (no 38) and from Wrexham via Dolgellau (no 94)

Barmouth is the major resort on the Cambrian Coast. St John's Church should have had its foundation stone laid by Queen Victoria in 1889, but her daughter Princess Beatrice was sent instead as the Non-Conformists were outraged by the continuing establishment of the Church in Wales and the tithes which they had to pay. The Frenchman's Grave is that of August Guyard, a friend of Victor Hugo and of John Ruskin, whose Guild of St George was presented with property here. Dinas Oleu was the first land given to the National Trust, in 1895 by Mrs Talbot.

ROUTE 11

BWLCH Y LLAN

2¼ miles

Moderate

G.R. SH619165
O.S. Outdoor Leisure map 18
Snowdonia - Harlech & Bala areas
or map 23 Snowdonia -
Cadair Idris area

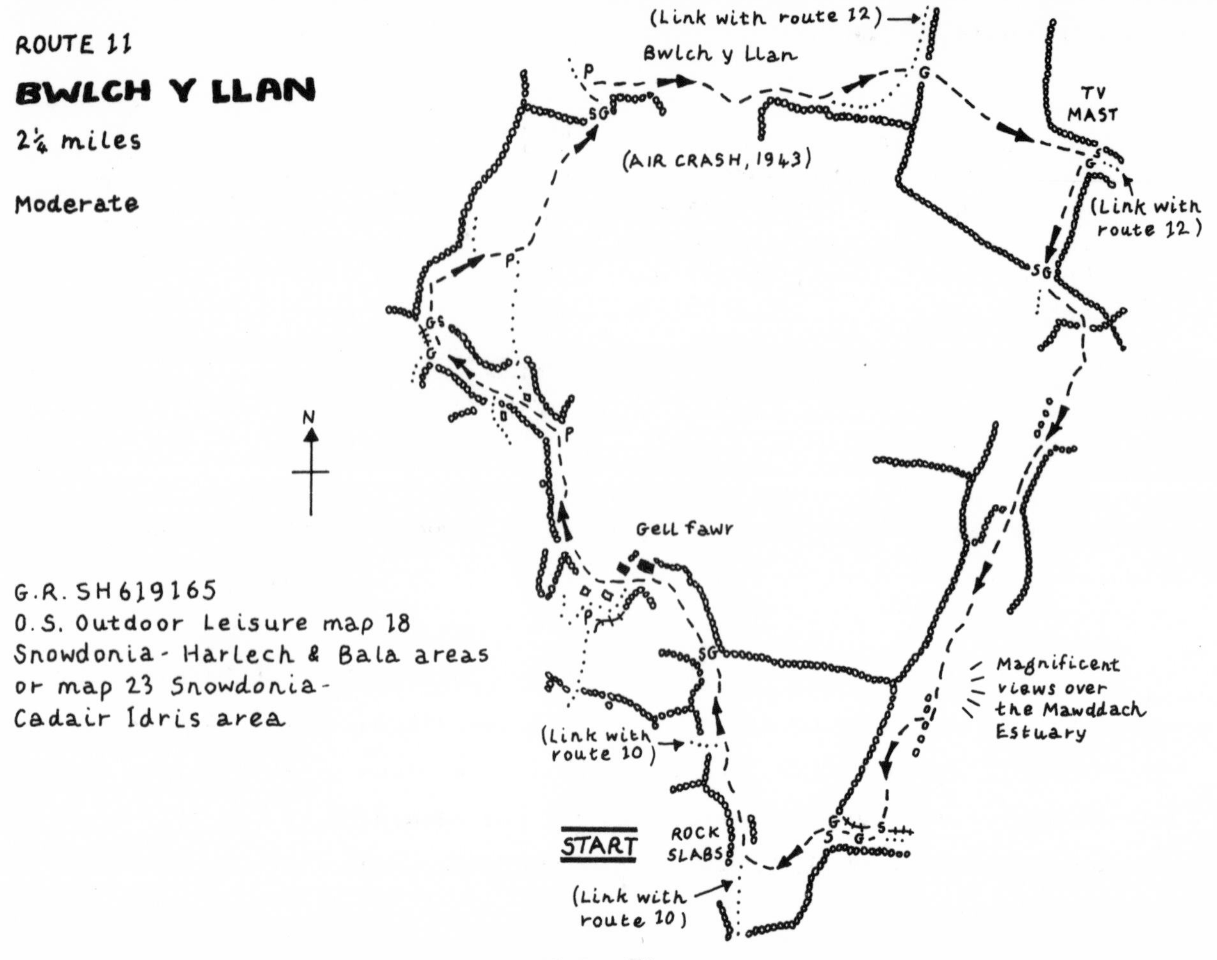

Route 11 **Bwlch y Llan**

The only way you can join this walk is to link it with route 10 (Barmouth). The Rock Slabs make an easily identifiable start and will probably be crowded with climbers. See route 10 (Barmouth) for details of public transport and car parking.

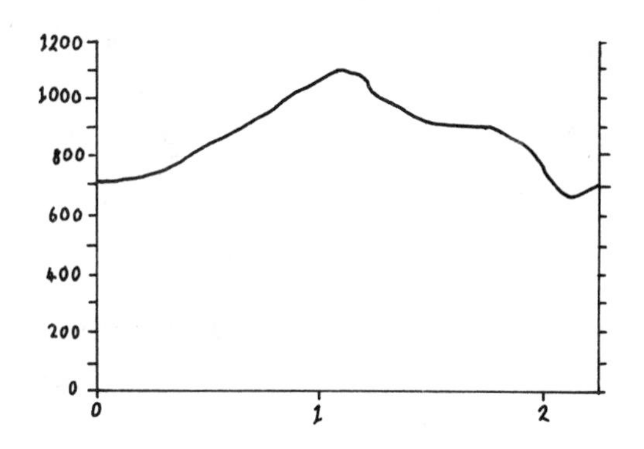

You may be daunted by the steep climb from Barmouth, but having made it you'll find it hard to leave this rugged, beautiful, wilderness and will find the courage to extend route 10 by linking it with this one and even with route 12. Bwlch y Llan was the scene of a tragedy on 26th/27th December 1943 when an Avro Anson attached to 9 Observers Advanced Flying Unit flew into the hill in low cloud. The aircraft was on a routine navigation exercise and was returning to its base at nearby RAF Llandwrog. All four of the crew were killed.

ROUTE 12

CERRIG ARTHUR

2¼ miles

Moderate

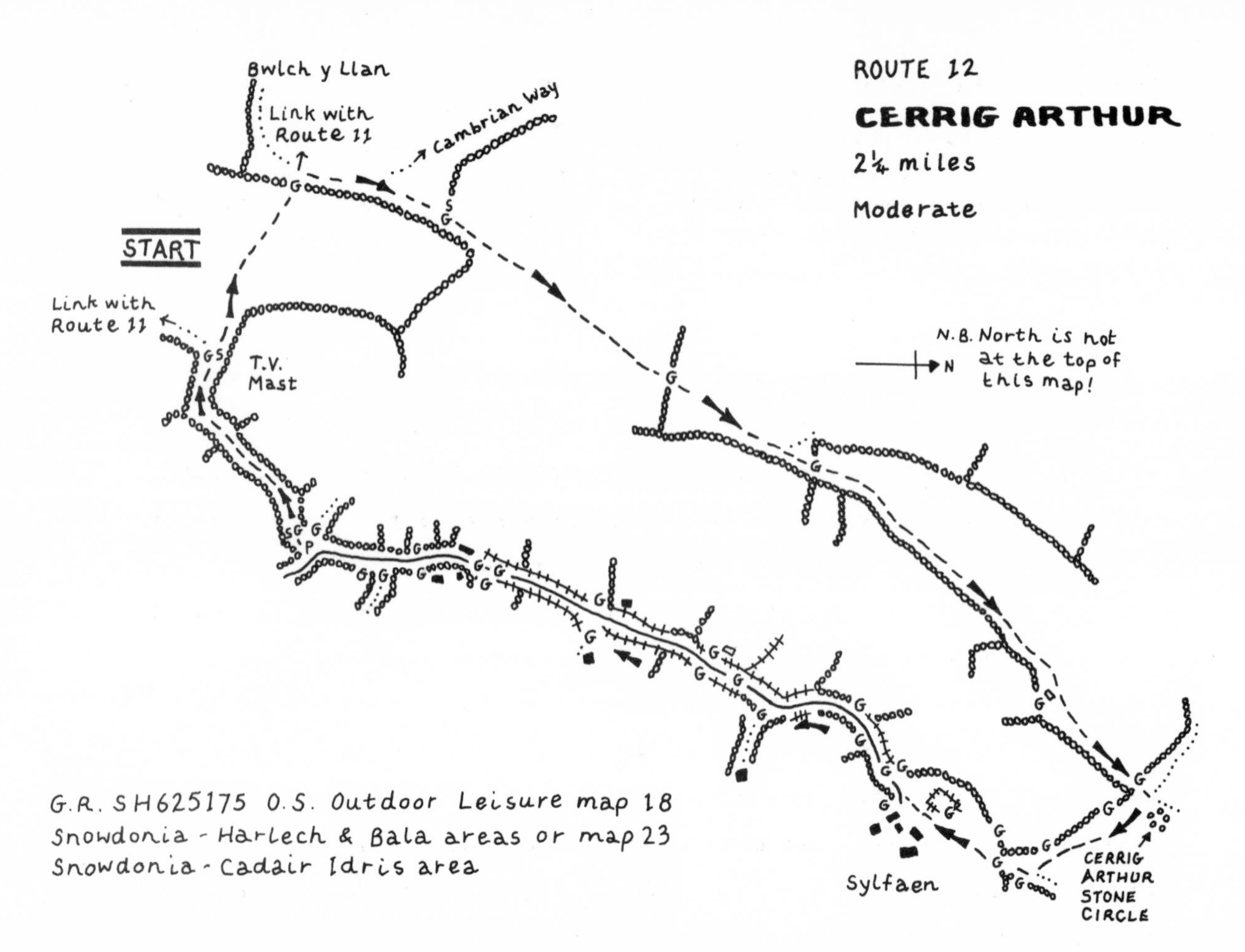

G.R. SH625175 O.S. Outdoor Leisure map 18 Snowdonia - Harlech & Bala areas or map 23 Snowdonia - Cadair Idris area

Route 12 **Cerrig Arthur**

Despite the access road to Sylfaen, there is nowhere to park a car. Join this walk by linking it with routes 10 and 11 (Barmouth and Bwlch y Llan).

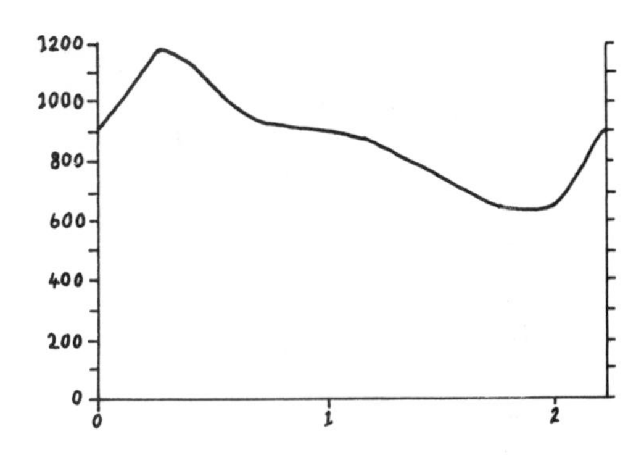

The views alone make such a trek worthwhile, with Cadair Idris (2928ft) easily identified across the Mawddach Estuary to the south and Diffwys rising to 2462ft to the north-north-east. You know you are in the Rhinogs now! A superb mountain ridge goes north from here and experienced ramblers can follow Tony Drake's 'Cambrian Way' along it. This long distance route (274 miles from Cardiff to Conwy) veers left along a courtesy path north of Bwlch y Llan. Only a few stones are left of Cerrig Arthur stone circle but the levelled platform is obvious. The axis of the ring, which has a radius of nearly 10 megalithic yards, points south-south-east to where the extreme southerly rising of the moon would have taken place in 1700 BC. There are small notches on the skyline in this area.

ROUTE 13

BONTDDU

2 miles

Moderate

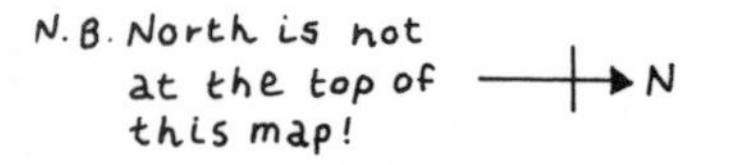

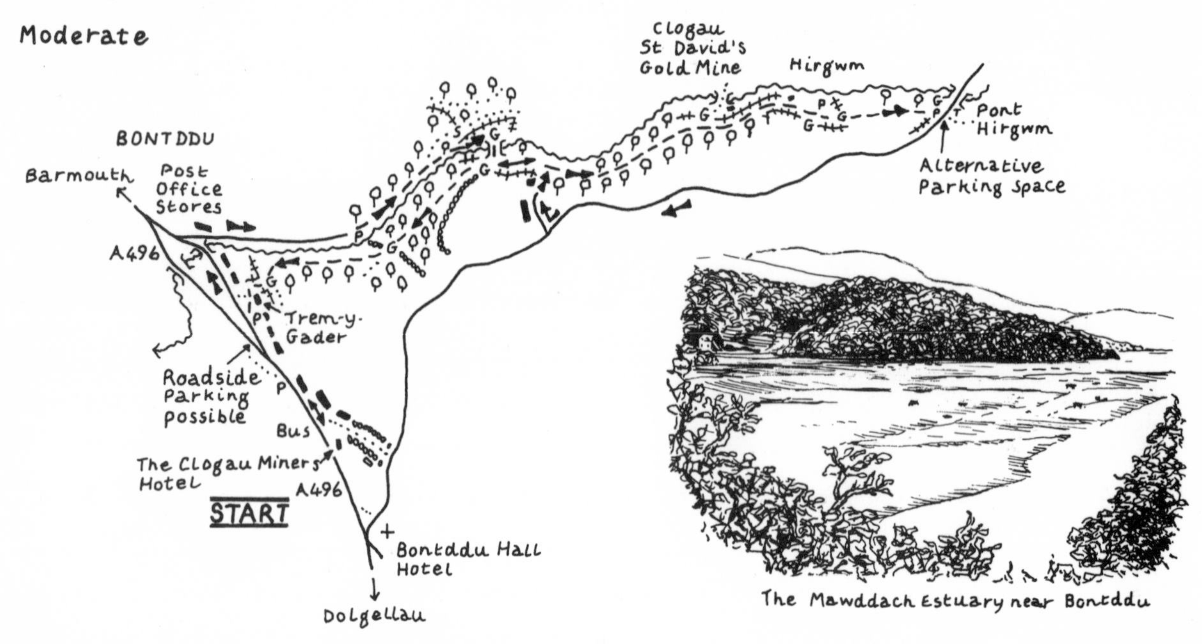

The Mawddach Estuary near Bontddu

G.R. SH672189 O.S. Outdoor Leisure map 18
Snowdonia: Harlech & Bala areas

Route 13, **Bontddu**

Parking:
There is space for roadside parking near the start (try the old road) and halfway around this route at Pont Hirgwm.

Public Transport:
Bus no 94 (Barmouth-Wrexham) stops at the Clogau Miners Hotel, Bontddu.

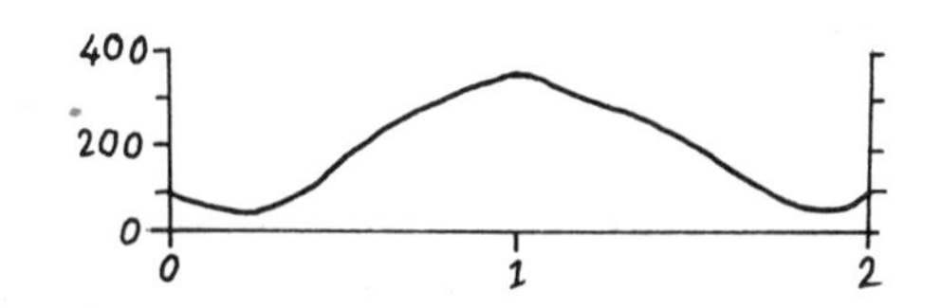

This area was famous for its gold mines during the latter half of the 19th century and the early years of the 20th century. Indeed, gold mining still took place here in the 1980 s. The mine passed on this walk is now disused. A scheme to open it as a tourist attraction was defeated in the late 1980 s. The local employment would have been welcome but not the extra traffic and the chair lift, which would have caused the chopping down of many oak trees. This mine is on the St David's Lode and became the deep adit level of the Clogau Mine. The original St David's Mine was nearly a mile to the east-north-east. The trees frame views down the valley to the Mawddach estuary, with Cadair Idris in the background.

ROUTE 14

CYMER ABBEY

2¾ miles

Easy

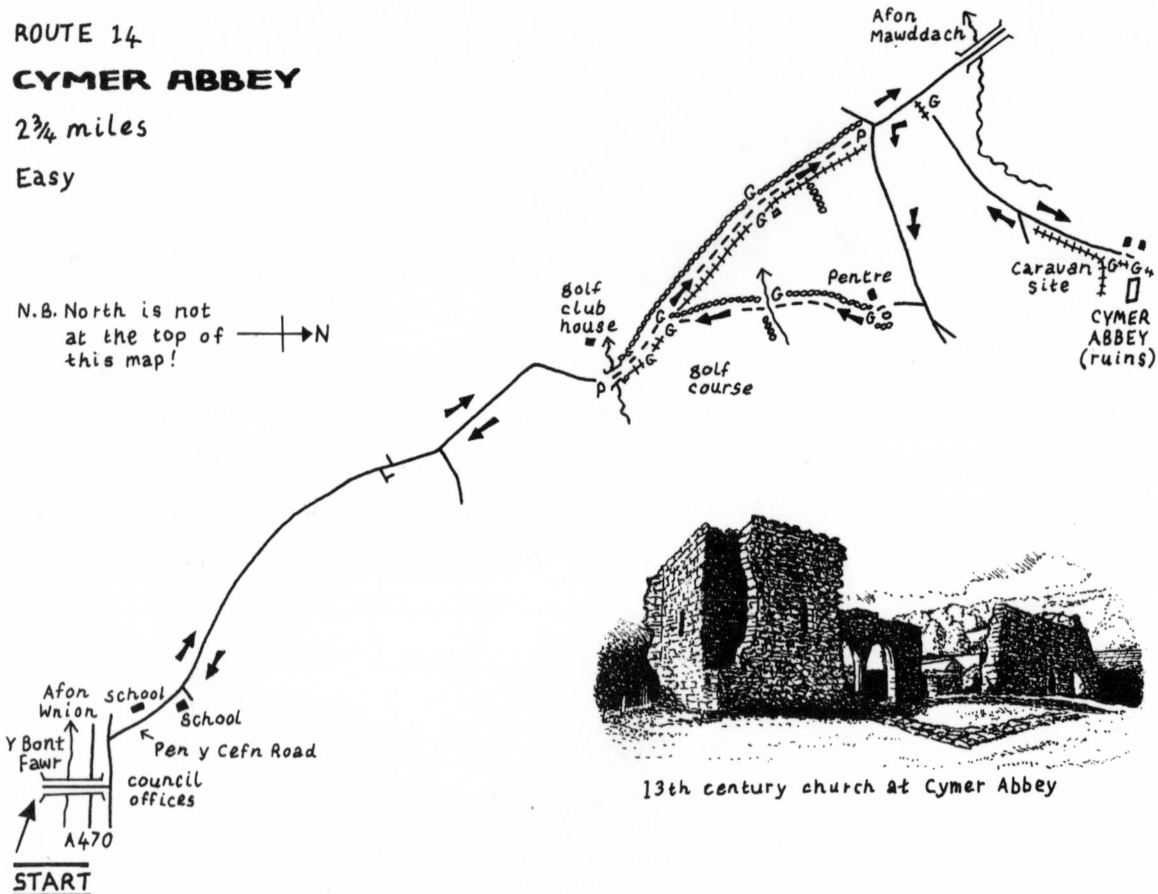

13th century church at Cymer Abbey

G.R. SH729180 O.S. Outdoor Leisure map 23 Snowdonia: Cadair Idris area.

Route 14, Cymer Abbey

Parking:
At the Marian, near Y Bont Fawr, Dolgellau.

Public Transport:
Dolgellau is at the hub of the Bws Gwynnedd network in Meirionnydd.

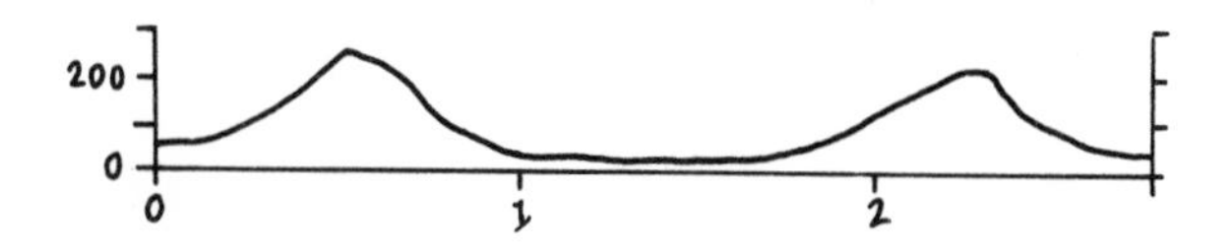

Y Bont Fawr (The Big Bridge) was built in 1683. The construction of the railway (now the A470 road) led to some rebuilding on the northern side in 1868. Dolgellau is the former county town of Meirionnydd, before the latter became part of Gwynedd in 1974. It is well provided with facilities, including a Snowdonia National Park Visitors' Centre and a Quaker Heritage Centre. A quiet lane leads to Cymer Abbey. This was founded by the Cistercians in either 1198 or 1199 and was a colony of the Abbey of Cwmhir in Powys. It was not a wealthy community, with a revenue of under £12 recorded in 1291. Most of the buildings dated from the early 13th century and the English wars and conquest seem to have halted expansion plans. The abbey was suppressed in 1536 and is now in the care of Cadw (admission fee; open Mar-Oct, Mon-Sat 9.30-6.30, Sun 2-6.30; Oct-Mar, Mon-Sat 9.30-4, Sun 2-4).

ROUTE 15

DOLGELLAU

3 miles

Moderate

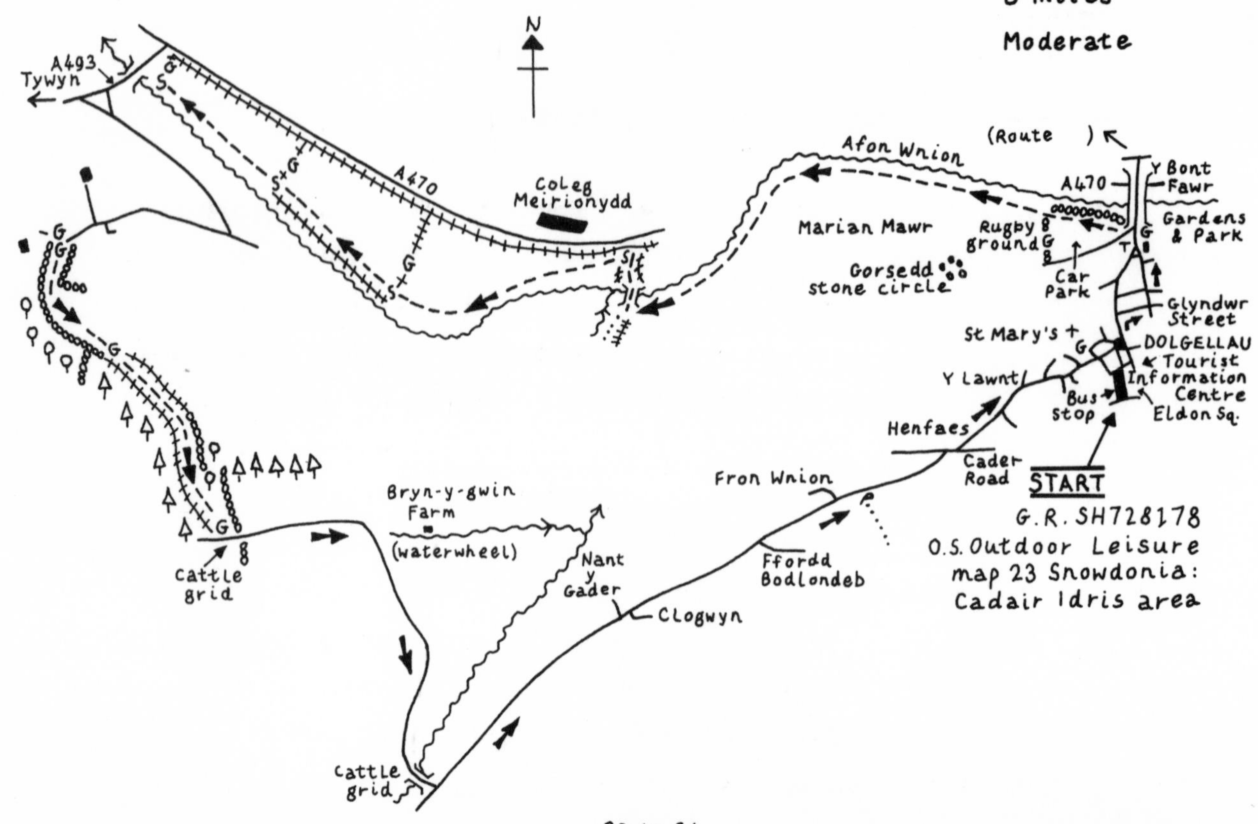

Route 15, Dolgellau

Parking:
Marian car park near
Y Bont Fawr

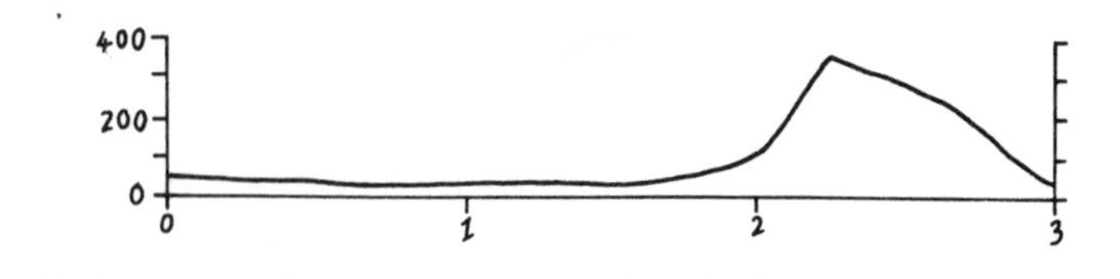

Public Transport:
Dolgellau is at the centre of the Bws Gwynedd network in Meirionydd. Buses stop in Eldon Square.

Dolgellau is a maze of grey granite and slate buildings separated by irregular narrow lanes which give the place character. The Ironmonger's (T.H.Roberts) near Glyndŵr Street is built on the site of the building where Owain Glyndŵr held court in 1404, before calling his parliament in Machynlleth. In Dolgellau on May 10th 1404, Glyndŵr announced that Gruffydd Young, Archdeacon of Meirioneth and John de Hamer were his ambassadors in negotiations with the French king, Charles VII. St Mary's church has an effigy of a 14th century knight (Meurig ap Ynyr Fychan from Nannau) and wooden pillars which were brought by oxen-drawn carts from the forests of Mawddwy. The stone circle is modern, having been erected for the Royal National Eisteddfod in 1949. The water-wheel at Bryn-y-gwin Farm is also recent, dating from 1984. There was a water-wheel here before, perhaps for an early 19th century fulling mill.

ROUTE 16

A QUAKER TRAIL

2 miles

Strenuous

Bryn-Mawr

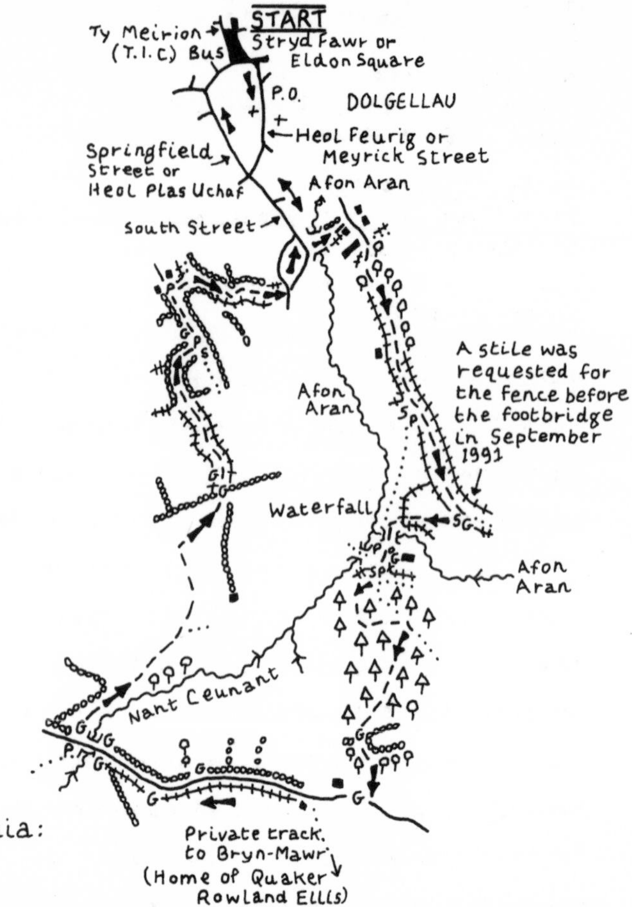

G.R. SH728178

O.S. Outdoor Leisure map 23, Snowdonia: Cadair Idris area

Route 16, **A Quaker Trail**

Parking:
Marian car park, Dolgellau (near Y Bont Fawr).

Public Transport:
Dolgellau is at the centre of the Bws Gwynedd network in Meirionnydd. Buses stop in Eldon Square.

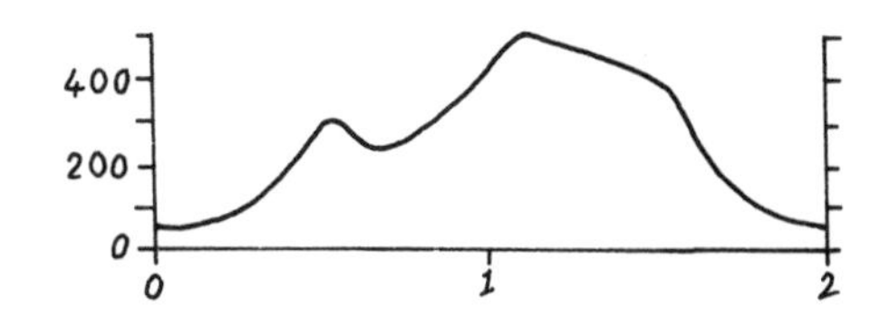

Marian Eames, the novelist and playwright, opened the Quaker Heritage Centre in the new Snowdonia National Park Visitor Centre at Ty Meirion in Dolgellau's Eldon Square on Friday 13th September 1991 - Quakers can't be superstitious! It marks the heroism of local Quakers in the 17th century, persecuted for listening to 'the Inner Light' rather than conforming to church creeds and rites. One, Robert Owen of Dolserau, spent five and a half years in a damp prison for refusing to swear the Oath of Allegiance because Jesus taught him not to swear. Another was Rowland Ellis of Bryn-mawr, who was threatened with being hanged, drawn and quartered for not taking an oath. He joined other Welsh Quakers in America, where his new farm was called Bryn-mawr. Later this name was acquired by the famous women's college in Pennsylvania.

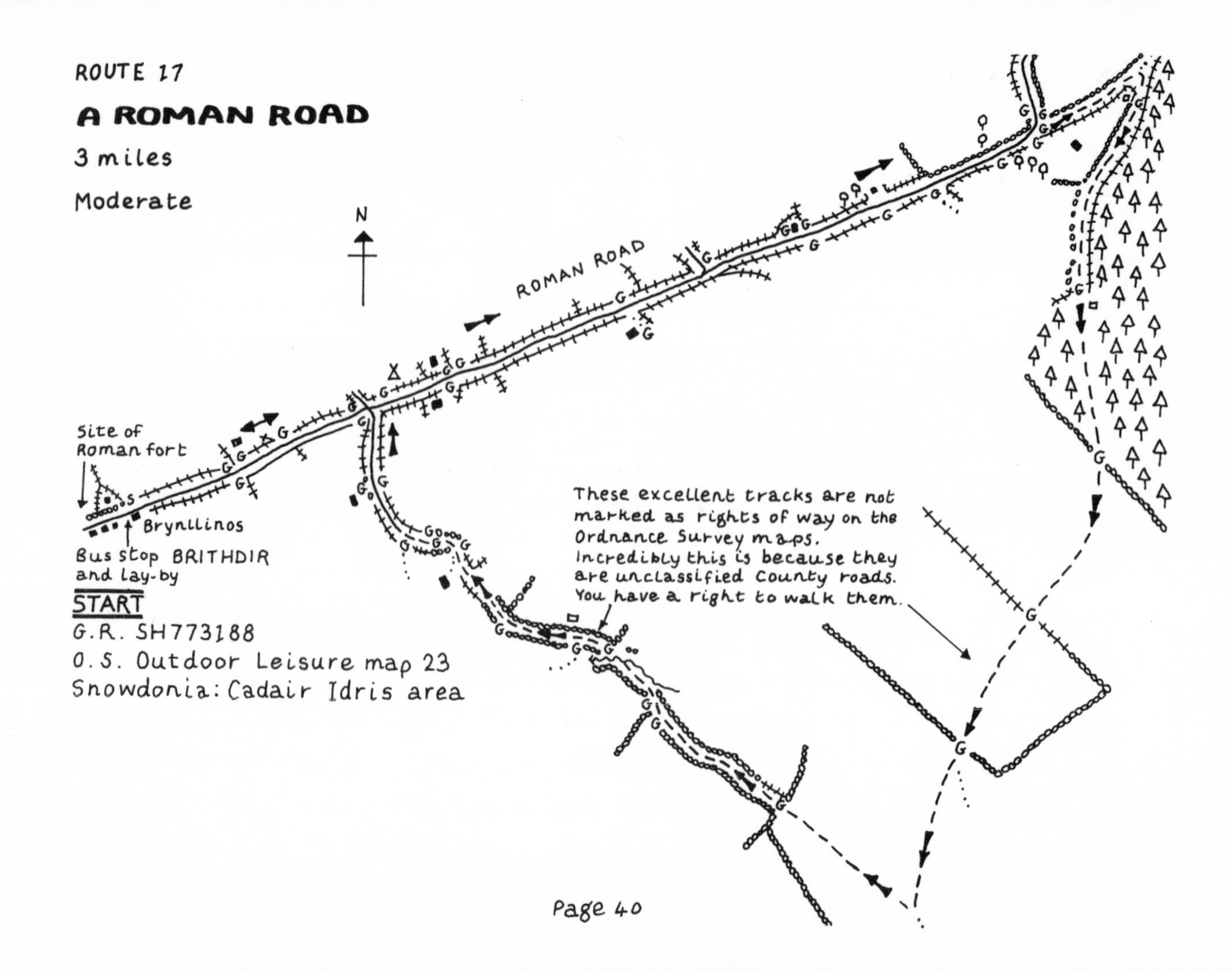
ROUTE 17
A ROMAN ROAD
3 miles
Moderate
N
ROMAN ROAD
Site of Roman fort
Brynllinos
Bus stop BRITHDIR and lay-by
START
G.R. SH773188
O.S. Outdoor Leisure map 23
Snowdonia: Cadair Idris area
These excellent tracks are not marked as rights of way on the Ordnance Survey maps. Incredibly this is because they are unclassified County roads. You have a right to walk them.

Route 17 A Roman Road

Parking:
There is a lay-by at the start of this walk in Brithdir.

Public Transport:
Brithdir is served infrequently by bus no 33 (becoming 27) running between Dolgellau and Dinas Mawddwy.

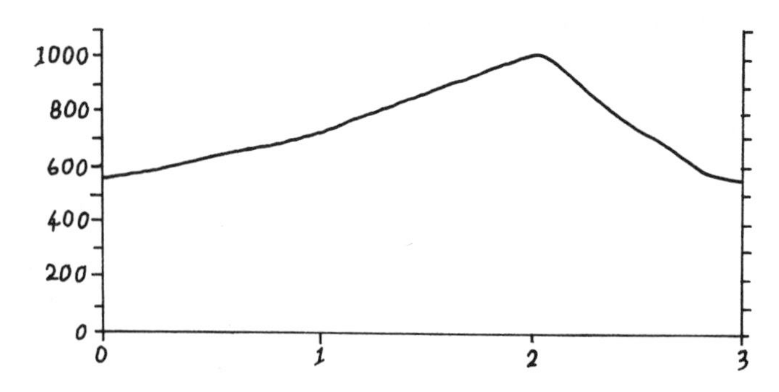

The Romans built a fort at Brithdir to mark an important road junction. Sarn Helen comes this way on its route between Carmarthen in south Wales and Caerhun (near Conwy) in north Wales. The road from Wroxeter via Mallwyd terminates here, perhaps along the descending unclassified county road near the end of this walk. The road to Chester is the one this route starts by following. These roads are actually much older than the Romans, as an excavation of a site in Brithdir in the summer of 1991 may suggest. They provide excellent access to wild moorland with fine views. The Arans rise in the east, Cadair Idris dominates the south, the Rhinogs can be seen to the west, while Rhobell Fawr lies to the north. What more could you ask for?

ROUTE 18

CWM CYWARCH

2 miles

Easy

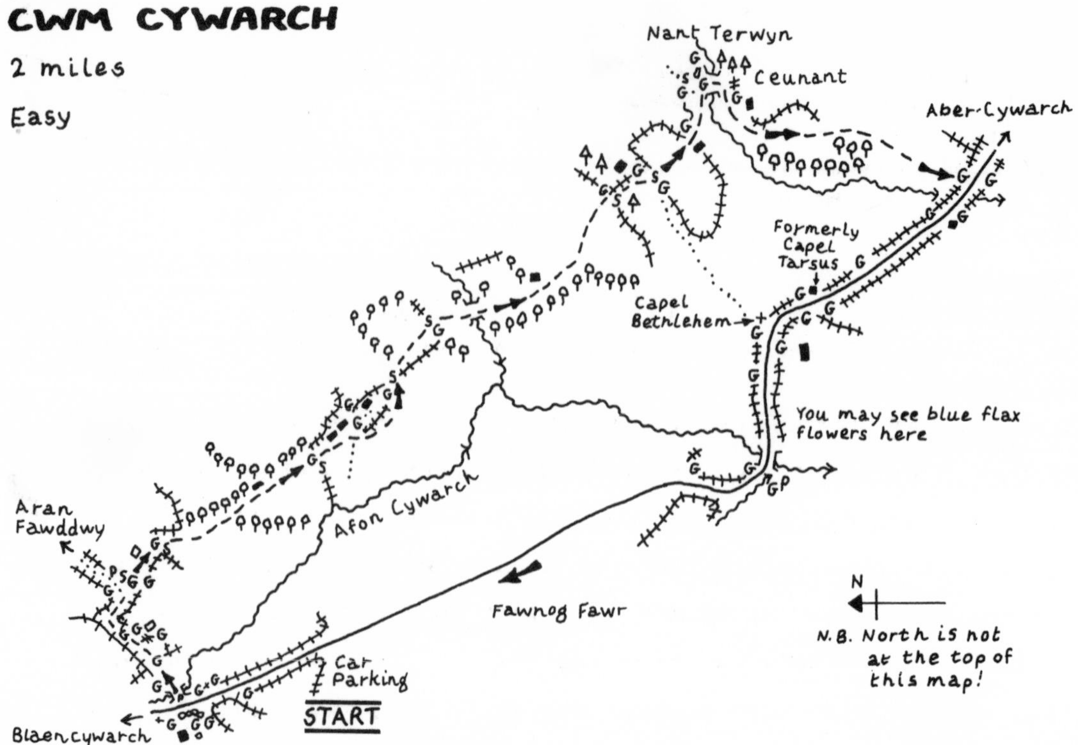

START

G.R. SH853185

O.S. Outdoor Leisure map 23 Snowdonia: Cadair Idris area

Route 18, Cwm Cywarch

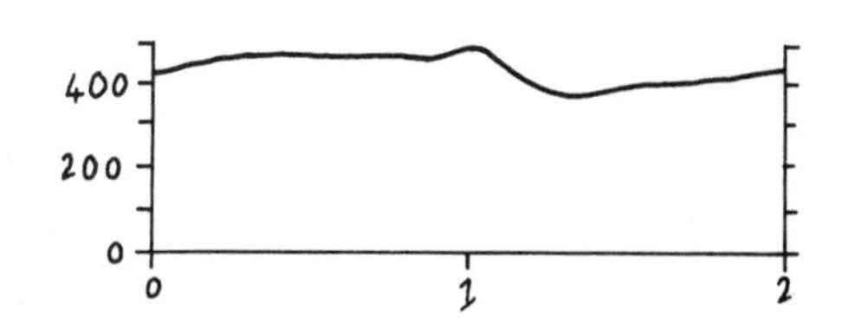

Parking:
There is a popular but unofficial car park at the top of the common in Cwm Cywarch. Snowdonia National Park intends to provide an official car park soon. This should be signposted.

Public Transport:
The nearest bus stop is in Dinas Mawddwy (no 27 from Dolgellau and no S18 from Machynlleth), adding an extra two miles each way to this route.

Cwm Cywarch is one of the most beautiful and inspiring valleys in Wales. It is hemmed in on three sides by mountains, with the rugged rocks of Craig Cywarch overlooking the car parking area. These attract rock climbers, who have a mountain club hut at Bryn Hafod. Here too is the start for the ascent of the 2971ft peak of Aran Fawddwy. Our route contents itself with the views from the floor of this valley whose name means flax valley. Some flax flowers can still be seen, indicating that flax must once have been grown here. Blaencywarch, higher up the valley, was famous for its lead mines, located near Bryn Hafod.

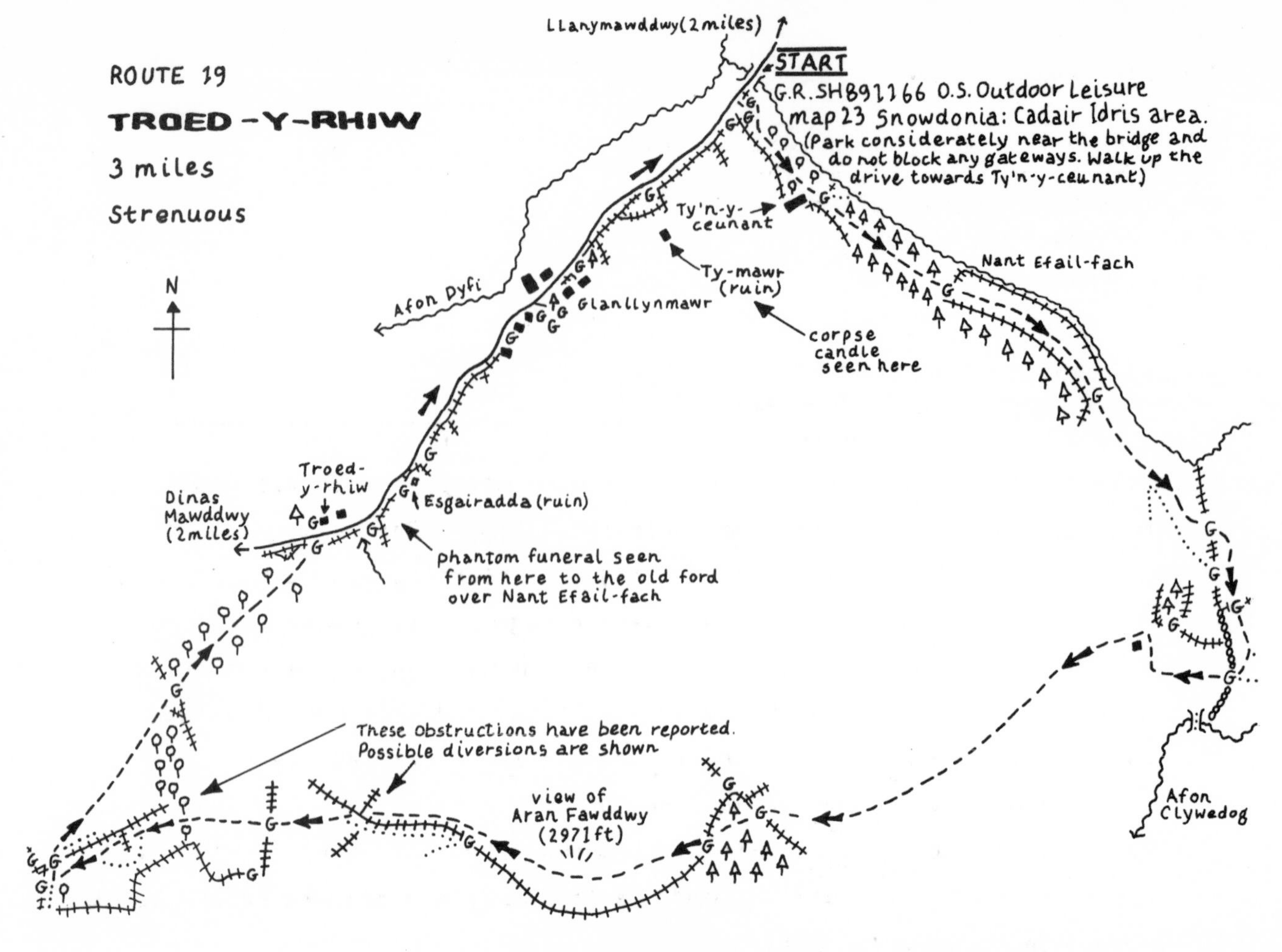
ROUTE 19
TROED-Y-RHIW
3 miles
Strenuous
Llanymawddwy (2 miles)
START
G.R. SH891166 O.S. Outdoor Leisure map 23 Snowdonia: Cadair Idris area.
(Park considerately near the bridge and do not block any gateways. Walk up the drive towards Ty'n-y-ceunant)
N
Afon Dyfi
Ty'n-y-ceunant
Ty-mawr (ruin)
Glanllynmawr
Nant Efail-fach
corpse candle seen here
Troed-y-rhiw
Esgairadda (ruin)
Dinas Mawddwy (2miles)
phantom funeral seen from here to the old ford over Nant Efail-fach
These obstructions have been reported. Possible diversions are shown
view of Aran Fawddwy (2971ft)
Afon Clywedog

Route 19, Troed-y-rhiw

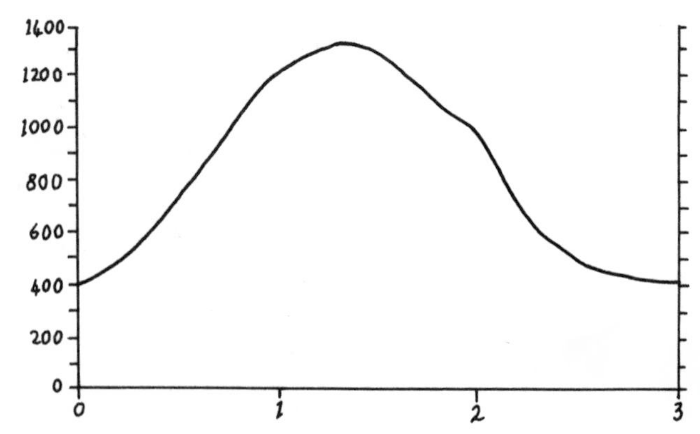

Parking:
Near the bridge across Nant Efail-fach on the minor road south of the Afon Dyfi between Dinas Mawddwy and Llanymawddwy.

Public Transport:
The nearest bus stop is in Dinas Mawddwy (no 27 from Dolgellau and no S18 from Machynlleth). Add an extra two miles each way between Dinas Mawddwy and Troed-y-rhiw.

This beautiful walk is also distinguished by a story of a corpse candle (cannwyll corff) and of a phantom funeral, or toili. One moonlit night, Margaret Lewis of Llwyngwilym (died 1958) was returning from a visit to a sick lady at Troed-y-rhiw when, just before Esgairadda, she saw two robed clergymen walking ahead of her towards Llanymawddwy church. Next morning she heard that the sick lady had died just after she left her. She had seen the funeral cortege as it did actually take place a few days later.
The corpse candle was seen going from Ty-mawr to Ty'n-y-ceunant, where it stopped before continuing towards Llanymawddwy. Two days later a lady died in childbirth at Ty-mawr and her body rested in Ty'n-y-ceunant before being taken to Llanymawddwy for burial.

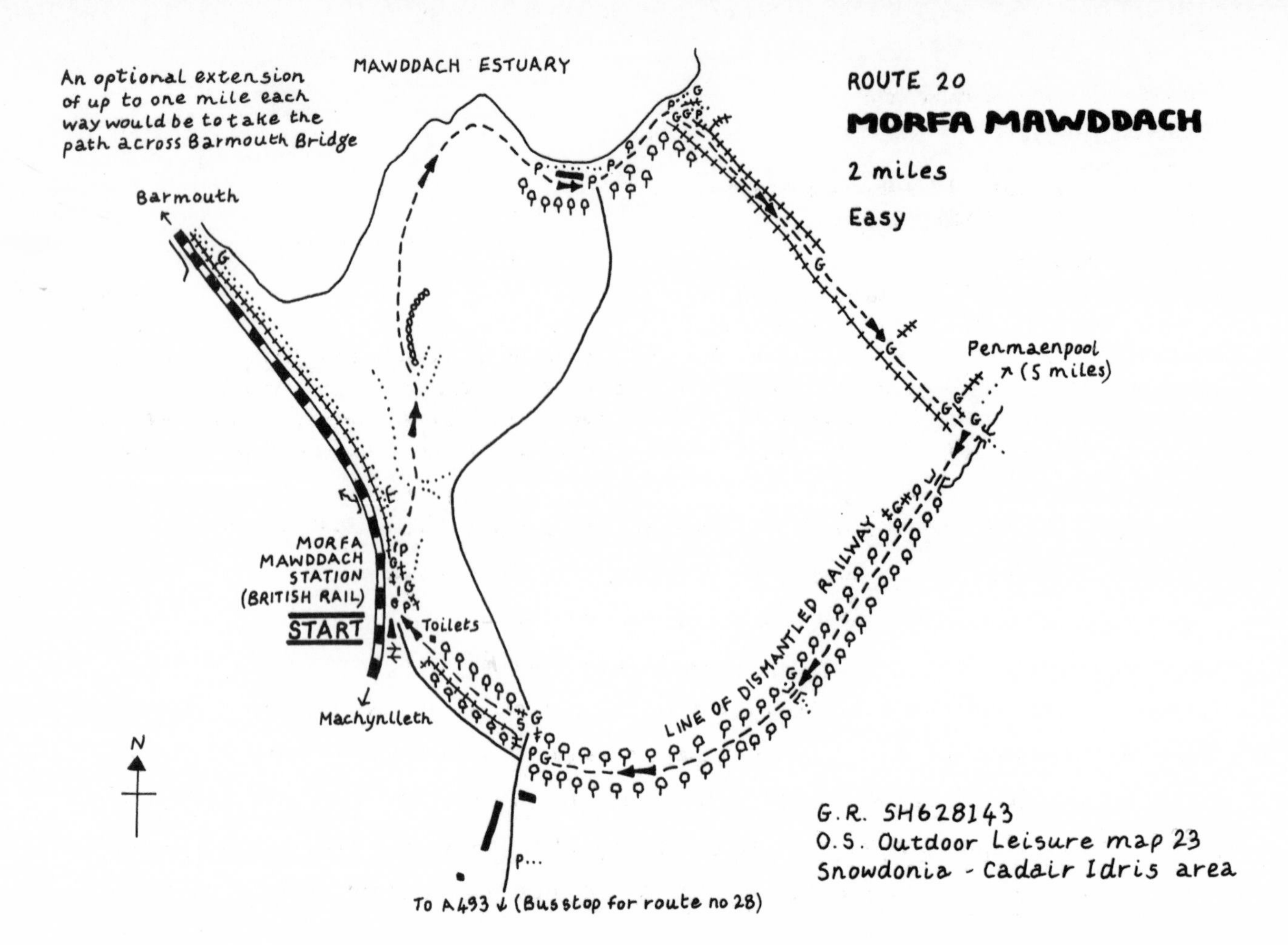
MAWDDACH ESTUARY
An optional extension of up to one mile each way would be to take the path across Barmouth Bridge
ROUTE 20
MORFA MAWDDACH
2 miles
Easy
Barmouth
Penmaenpool
(5 miles)
MORFA MAWDDACH STATION (BRITISH RAIL)
START
Toilets
Machynlleth
LINE OF DISMANTLED RAILWAY
N
G.R. SH628143
O.S. Outdoor Leisure map 23
Snowdonia - Cadair Idris area
To A493 (Busstop for route no 28)

Route 20, **Morfa Mawddach**

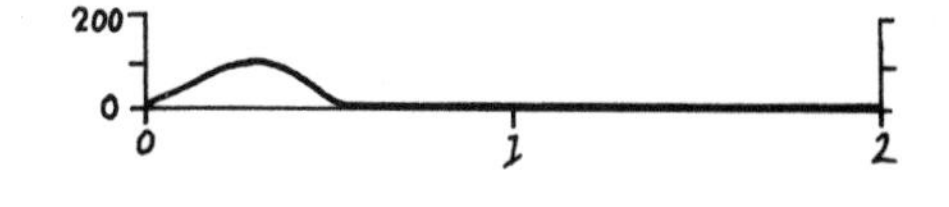

Parking:
There is a car park at the start, at Morfa Mawddach station.

Public Transport:
British Rail's Cambrian Coast Line (Machynlleth-Pwllheli) serves the halt at the start of this walk. Bus no 28 between Tywyn and Dolgellau passes the junction of the A493 and the access road to Morfa Mawddach station. You could also walk here from Barmouth (small toll) along the footbridge beside the railway bridge across the scenic Mawddach Estuary.

Tranquility is the theme of this walk, set beside the waters of the Mawddach near its mouth and including a section of old railway. The hustle and bustle of what was Barmouth Junction, marking where the line from Ruabon used by the holiday expresses from Manchester met the Cambrian Coast Line, has largely disappeared. You can still arrive at the start by train, however, even if you do have to request this halt. There is still the splendour of Barmouth Bridge, while the dismantled line has been turned into an enjoyable walk, most of it along the shore, all the way to Penmaenpool. You could catch the no 28 bus back from here.

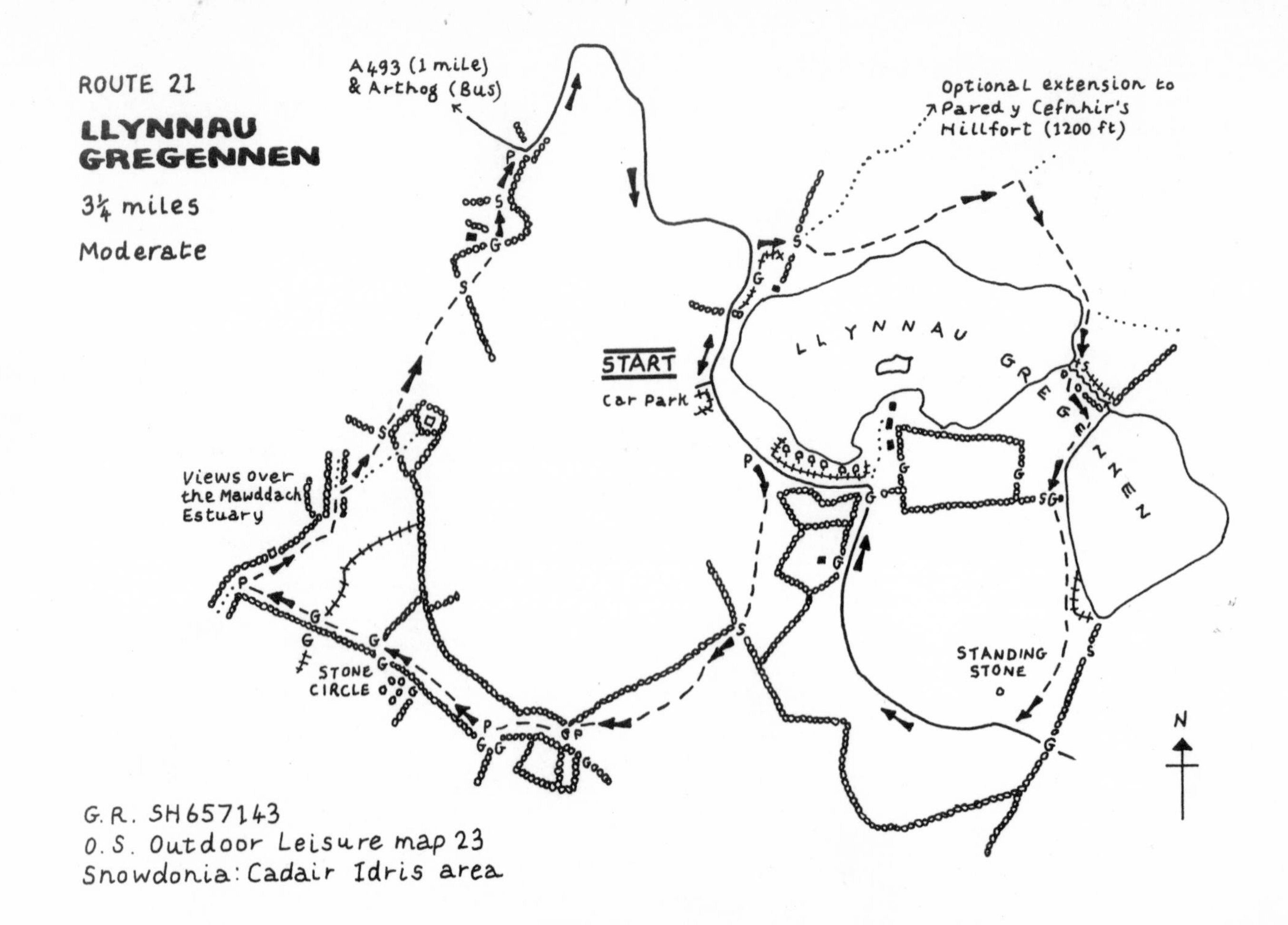
ROUTE 21
LLYNNAU GREGENNEN
3¼ miles
Moderate
A493 (1 mile) & Arthog (Bus)
Optional extension to Pared y Cefnhir's Hillfort (1200 ft)
START
Car Park
LLYNNAU GREGENNEN
Views over the Mawddach Estuary
STONE CIRCLE
STANDING STONE
N
G.R. SH657143
O.S. Outdoor Leisure map 23
Snowdonia: Cadair Idris area

Route 21, Llynnau Gregennen

Parking:
There is a National Trust car park at the start of this walk.

Public Transport:
The nearest bus stop is over one mile away at Arthog (no 28 between Tywyn and Dolgellau).

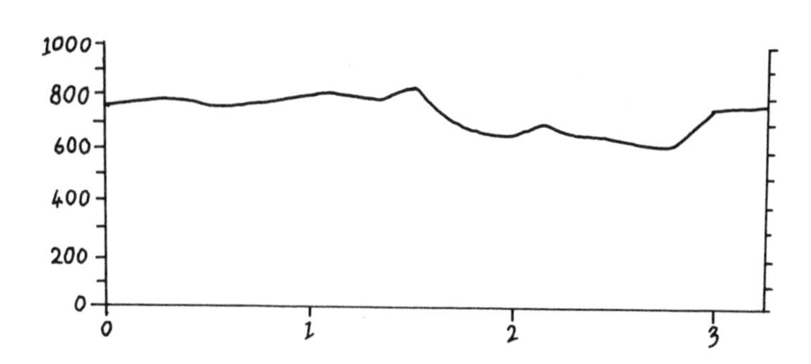

The wild grandeur of the Cregennan Lakes and their surroundings never fails to inspire those who trek up the foothills of the Cadair Idris range to see them. A strenuous but rewarding conclusion to this walk would be to ascend to 1200 feet for a close inspection of the ancient hillfort on the narrow ridge that forms the summit of Pared y Cefnhir. The views are likely to remain with you forever. Below lies the Mawddach estuary and Barmouth, while rising above is Cadair Idris and Tyrrau Mawr. This is a dramatic, sacred, spot. Prehistory is all around you, with a standing stone and a stone circle visited by this route. Allow plenty of time to contemplate and absorb the atmosphere of one of the most beautiful and special places in Snowdonia.

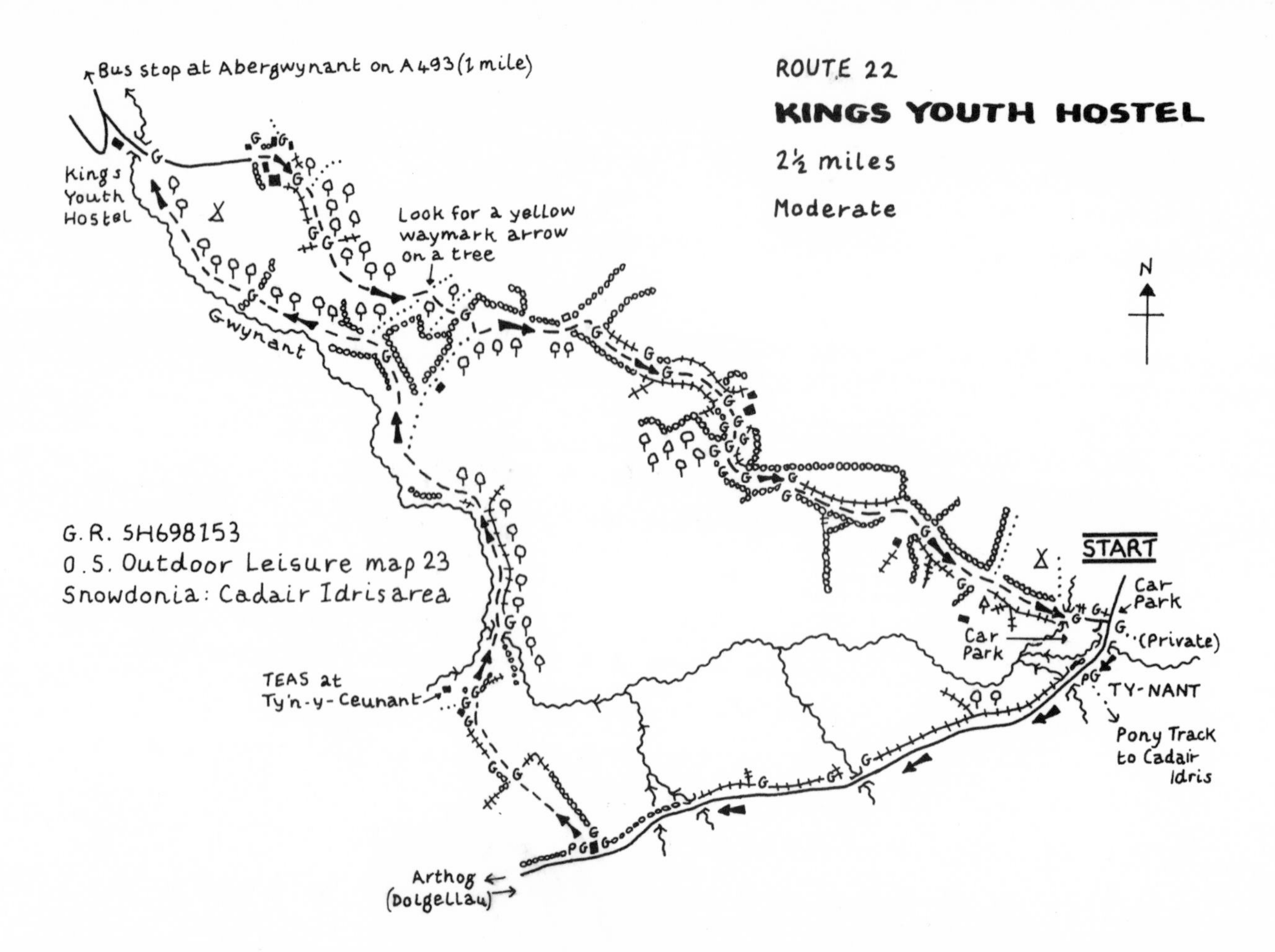
Bus stop at Abergwynant on A493 (1 mile)
ROUTE 22
KINGS YOUTH HOSTEL
2½ miles
Moderate
Kings Youth Hostel
Look for a yellow waymark arrow on a tree
N
Gwynant
G.R. SH698153
O.S. Outdoor Leisure map 23
Snowdonia: Cadair Idris area
START
Car Park
Car Park
(Private)
TY-NANT
TEAS at Ty'n-y-Ceunant
Pony Track to Cadair Idris
Arthog
(Dolgellau)

Route 22, **King's Youth Hostel**

Parking:
There is an official Snowdonia National Park car park at the start of this walk.

Public Transport:
The nearest bus stop is at Abergwynant (no 28 between Tywyn and Dolgellau). Add an extra mile each way and start at Kings Youth Hostel.

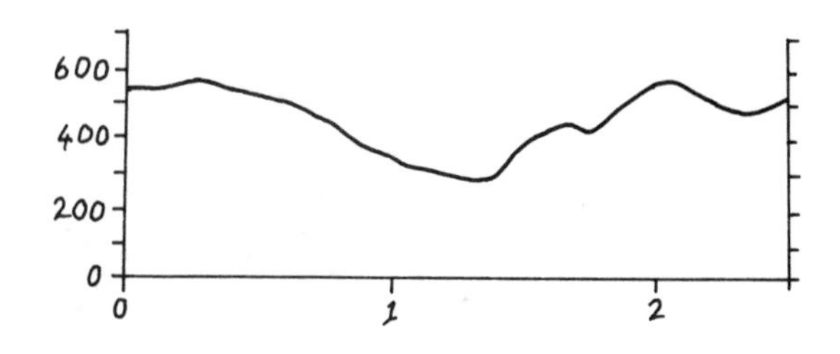

This is a delightful walk in the shadow of the 2928ft peak of Cadair Idris. This route will provide newcomers to walking with the experience recommended before tackling the mountains. It will also show you varied countryside with broadleaved trees and a tumbling mountain stream-with a magnificent backdrop. Enjoy a tea at Ty'n-y-ceunant and take a look at Kings Youth Hostel. This is one of many hostels which provide cheap, simple but comfortable accommodation for the young at heart (there is no upper age limit) throughout the British Isles and many countries in the world. Full details of the Youth Hostels Association are available (for an SAE) from the YHA, Trevelyan House, 8 St Stephen's Hill, St Albans, Hertfordshire, AL1 2DY.

ROUTE 23

THE DYFI VALLEY NORTH OF DINAS MAWDDWY

2½ miles

Easy

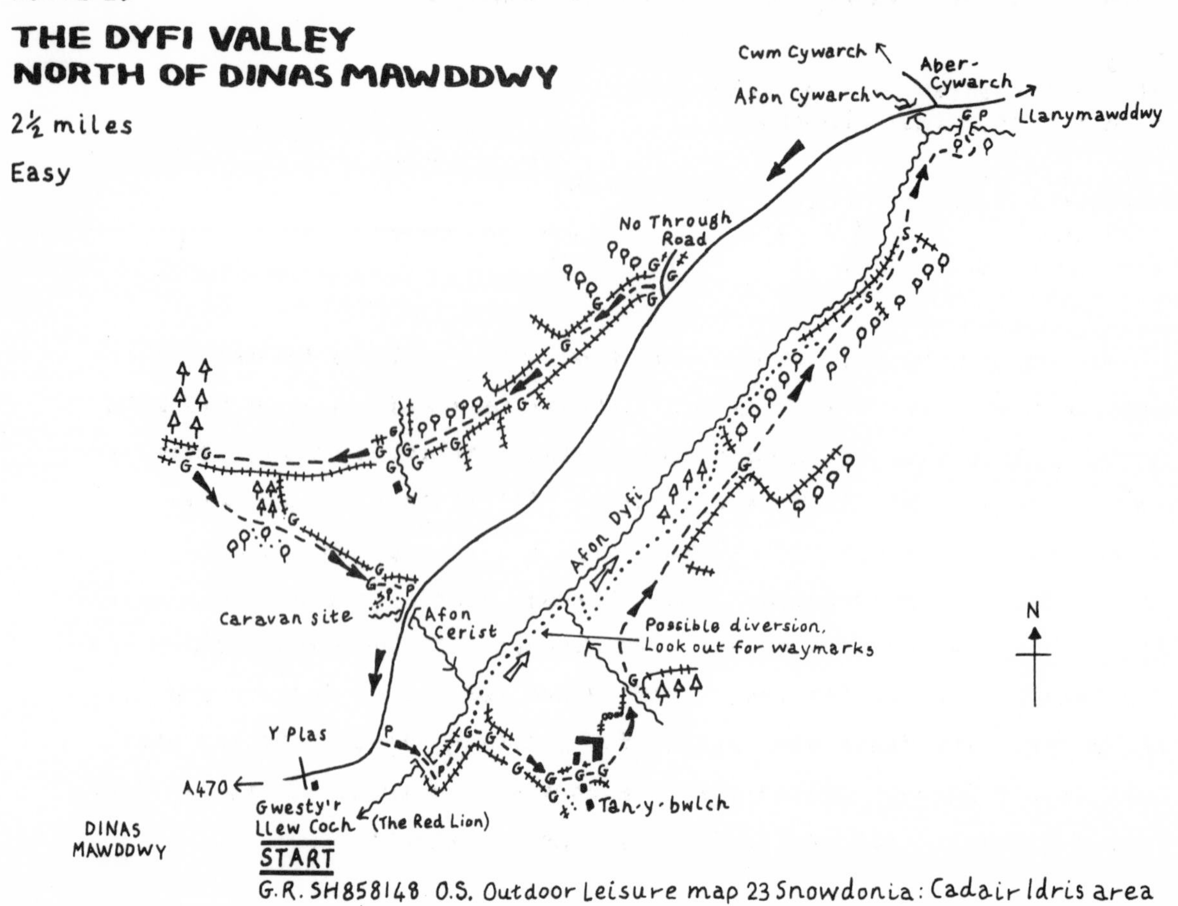

G.R. SH858148 O.S. Outdoor Leisure map 23 Snowdonia: Cadair Idris area

Route 23, **The Dyfi Valley North of Dinas Mawddwy**

Parking:
Outside the Gwesty'r Llew Coch or in Y Plas, Dinas Mawddwy.

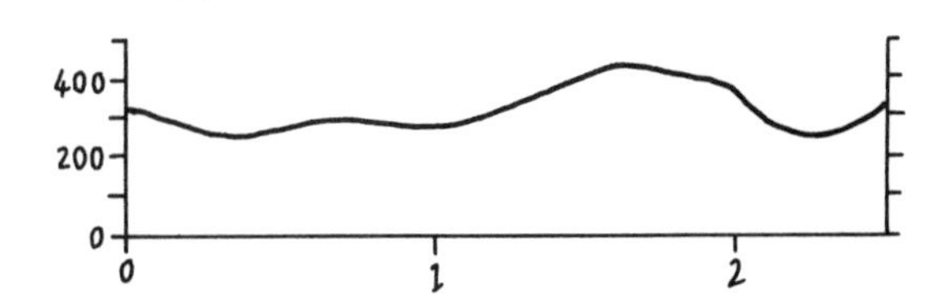

Public Transport:
Infrequent buses from Machynlleth (S18) and Dolgellau (27) stop near the Gwesty'r Llew Coch.

The Gwesty'r Llew coch is the oldest building in Dinas Mawddwy. There were several other inns here until the village's decline in the 20th century. Once this was a notorious enclave, attached to the county of Merionethshire after the Act of Union of 1536 to allow a firmer authority to wipe out its Red Bandits. This is a place used to independence, even granting itself borough status in the Middle Ages. Although not a properly constituted borough, its 'mayor' presided over 'The General Quarter Sessions of the Peace for the Borough of and city of Mawddwy' and fined many people for poaching salmon from the Afon Dyfi (River Dovey). Drunks were punished with a spell in the Feg Fawr (Great Fetter), reckoned much worse than any stocks.

ROUTE 24

PONT MINLLYN

2 miles

Moderate

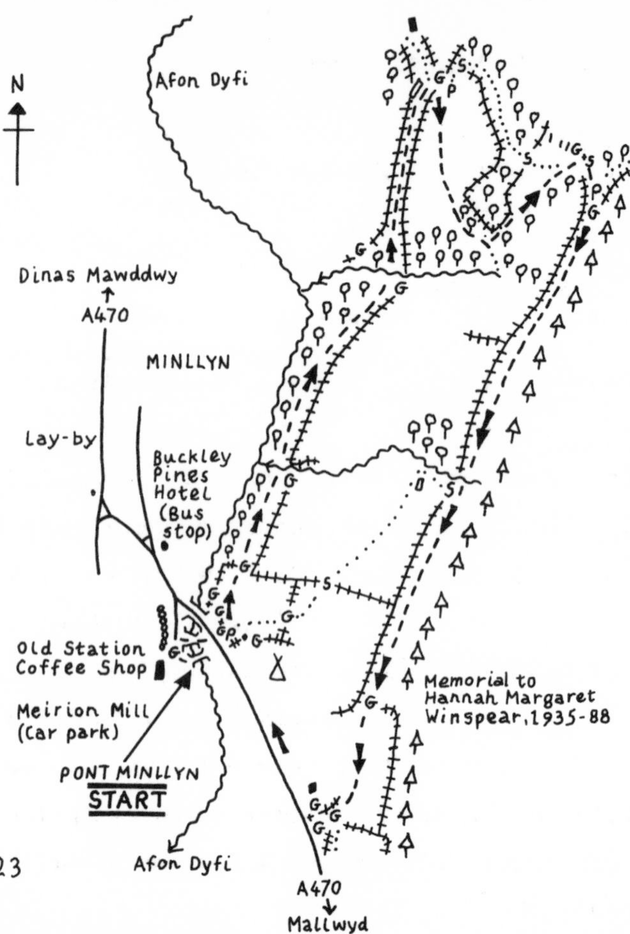

Pont Minllyn

G.R. SH859138 O.S. Outdoor Leisure map 23
Snowdonia: Cadair Idris area

Route 24, Pont Minllyn

Parking:
Meirion Mill (10am-5pm Mar-Oct)
or a lay-by on the A470 ¼ mile to
the north of the Meirion Mill.

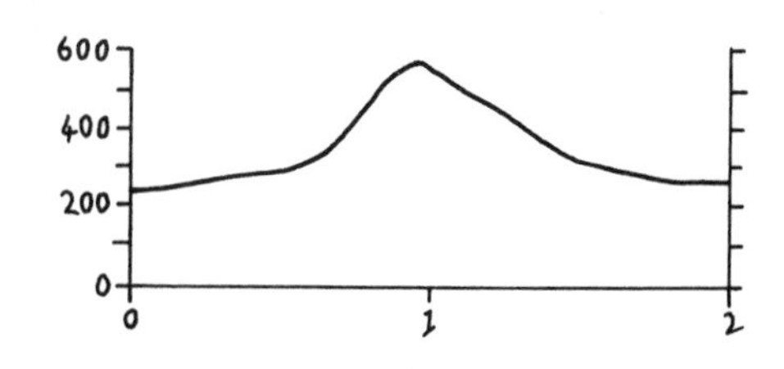

Public Transport:
The no 27 bus from Dolgellau and
the no S18 bus from Machynlleth stop
near the Buckley Pines Hotel, Minllyn.

Pont Minllyn is a packhorse bridge built under the direction of Dr John Davies, the rector of nearby St Tydecho's church, Mallwyd, in the 17th century. It marks an ancient ford. A Roman road between Wroxeter and Brithdir (near Dolgellau) crossed the Afon Dyfi here. The Mawddwy Railway terminated beside it from 1867 to its closure in 1951. Its old station is now a coffee shop, within the grounds of the Meirion Mill. Admission to the woollen mill and shop is free. Just to the south of here is Maes Camlan, the site of King Arthur's last battle at Camlan. A booklet about this is available in the mill shop.

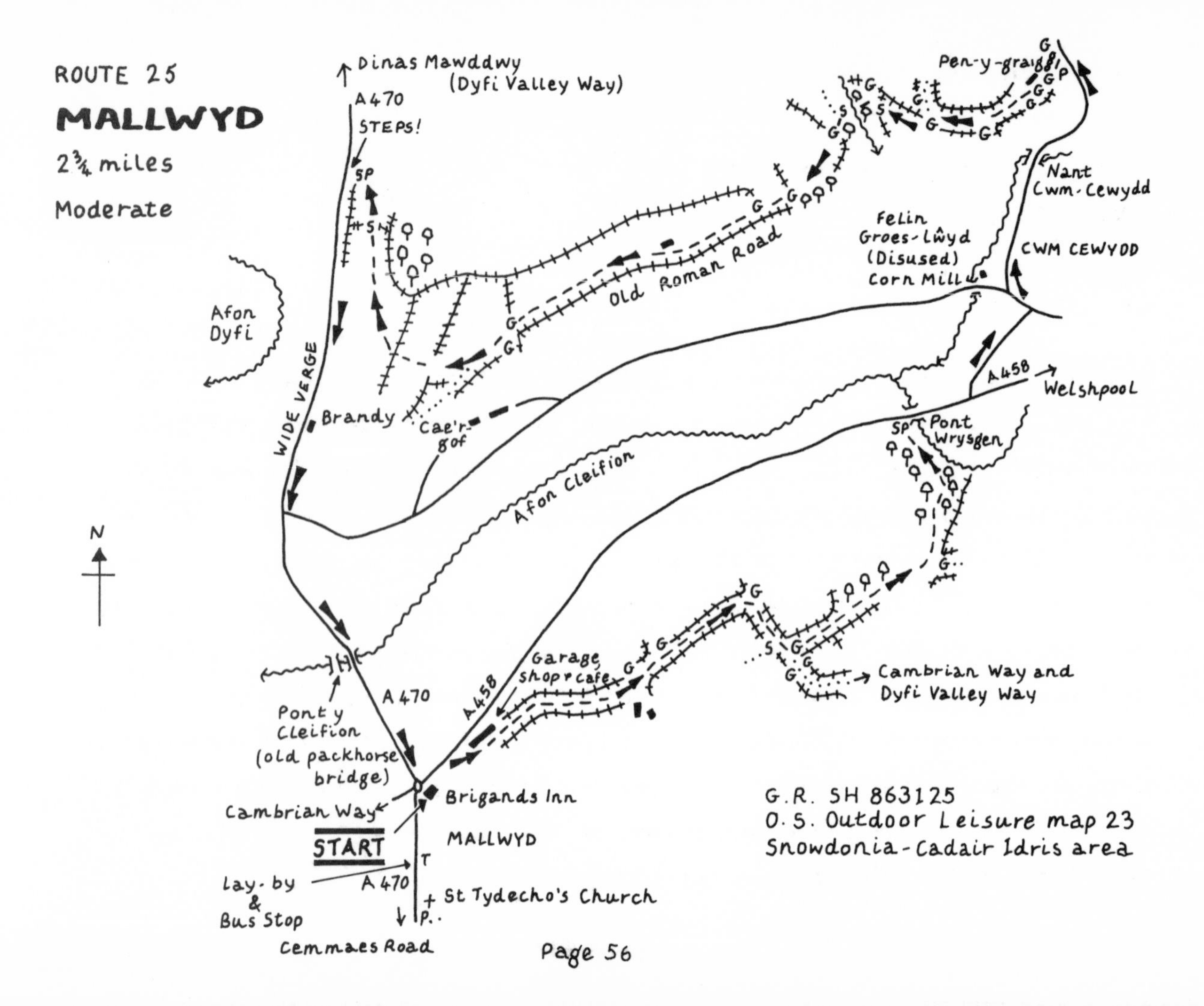

ROUTE 25
MALLWYD
2¾ miles
Moderate
Dinas Mawddwy
(Dyfi Valley Way)
A 470
STEPS!
SP
Afon Dyfi
WIDE VERGE
Brandy
Cae'r-gof
Old Roman Road
Pen-y-graig
Nant Cwm-Cewydd
Felin Groes-Lŵyd (Disused) Corn Mill
CWM CEWYDD
A458
Welshpool
Pont Wrysgen
Afon Cleifion
N
Pont y Cleifion (old packhorse bridge)
A 470
A458
Garage shop & cafe
Cambrian Way and Dyfi Valley Way
Brigands Inn
Cambrian Way
START
MALLWYD
Lay-by & Bus Stop
A 470
St Tydecho's Church
Cemmaes Road
G.R. SH 863125
O.S. Outdoor Leisure map 23
Snowdonia-Cadair Idris area

Parking:
There is a lay-by at the start.

Public Transport:
Mallwyd has infrequent bus services from Machynlleth (no S18) and Dolgellau (no 27).

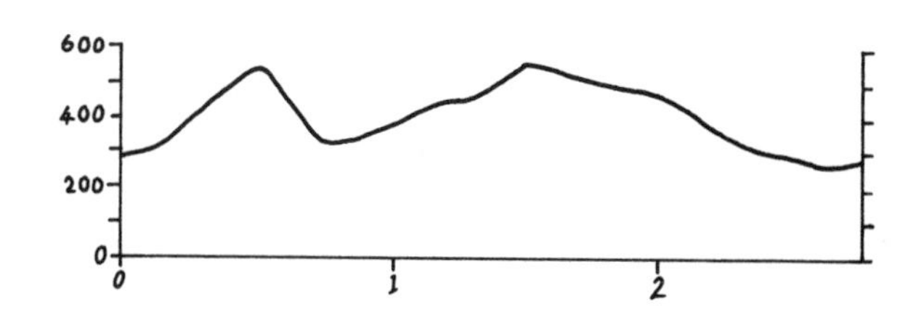

The Brigands Inn at Mallwyd is a reminder that this is bandit territory. The notorious Gwylliaid Cochion Mawddwy (Red Bandits of Mawddwy) held sway here for centuries. Most of them were wiped out in 1554 and 1555, but their memory was still potent when Thomas Pennant came this way in the 18th century and George Borrow in the 19th. Borrow recounts staying in this inn (formerly known as the Peniarth Arms) in his book 'Wild Wales'. (He rather enjoyed his stay). The Red Bandits may date from 1114, but the 'Mabinogion' story 'The Dream of Rhonabwy' records a red-freckled man (Cynwrig Frychgoch) from Mawddwy in the time of King Arthur. There was a Roman road (from Brithdir to Wroxeter) here then, while King Arthur's nephew St Tydecho founded the church in 520. The packhorse bridge over the Afon Cleifion dates from the 17th century.

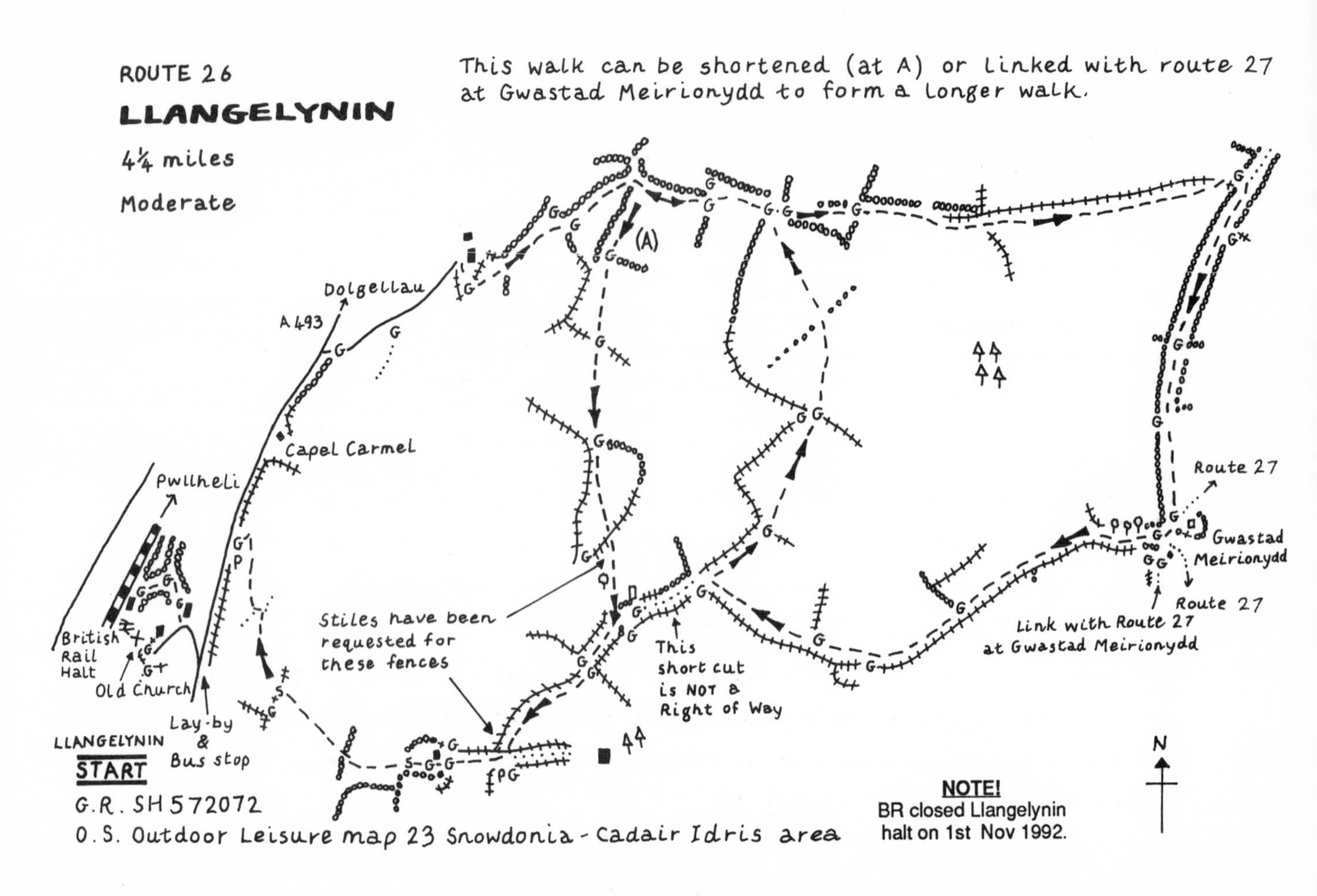
ROUTE 26
LLANGELYNIN
4¼ miles
Moderate
This walk can be shortened (at A) or linked with route 27 at Gwastad Meirionydd to form a longer walk.
Dolgellau
A 493
(A)
Capel Carmel
Pwllheli
British Rail Halt
Old Church
Lay-by & Bus stop
Stiles have been requested for these fences
This short cut is NOT a Right of Way
Route 27
Gwastad Meirionydd
Route 27
Link with Route 27 at Gwastad Meirionydd
LLANGELYNIN
START
G.R. SH 572072
O.S. Outdoor Leisure map 23 Snowdonia - Cadair Idris area
NOTE!
BR closed Llangelynin halt on 1st Nov 1992.
N

Route 26, Llangelynin

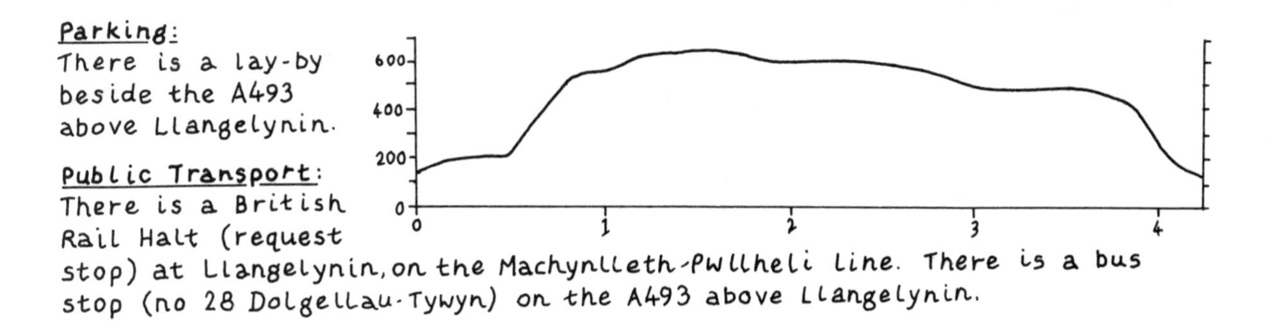

Parking:
There is a lay-by beside the A493 above Llangelynin.

Public Transport:
There is a British Rail Halt (request stop) at Llangelynin, on the Machynlleth-Pwllheli line. There is a bus stop (no 28 Dolgellau-Tywyn) on the A493 above Llangelynin.

Visit the old church of St Celynin to see a double horse bier on its north wall. Abram Wood, the 18th century 'King of the Gypsies', is buried near the porch. He died on 13th December 1799 and is believed to have been born in 1700. Rhys Evans, the prophet known as 'Arise Evans' was born here in 1607. Claiming to be Christ, he was thrown into Newgate Gaol by the Puritans. Having correctly predicted the Restoration of the monarchy, Evans was cured of a 'fungrous' growth on his nose by a touch from the hand of King Charles II.

ROUTE 27

LLANEGRYN CHURCH

3 miles

Moderate

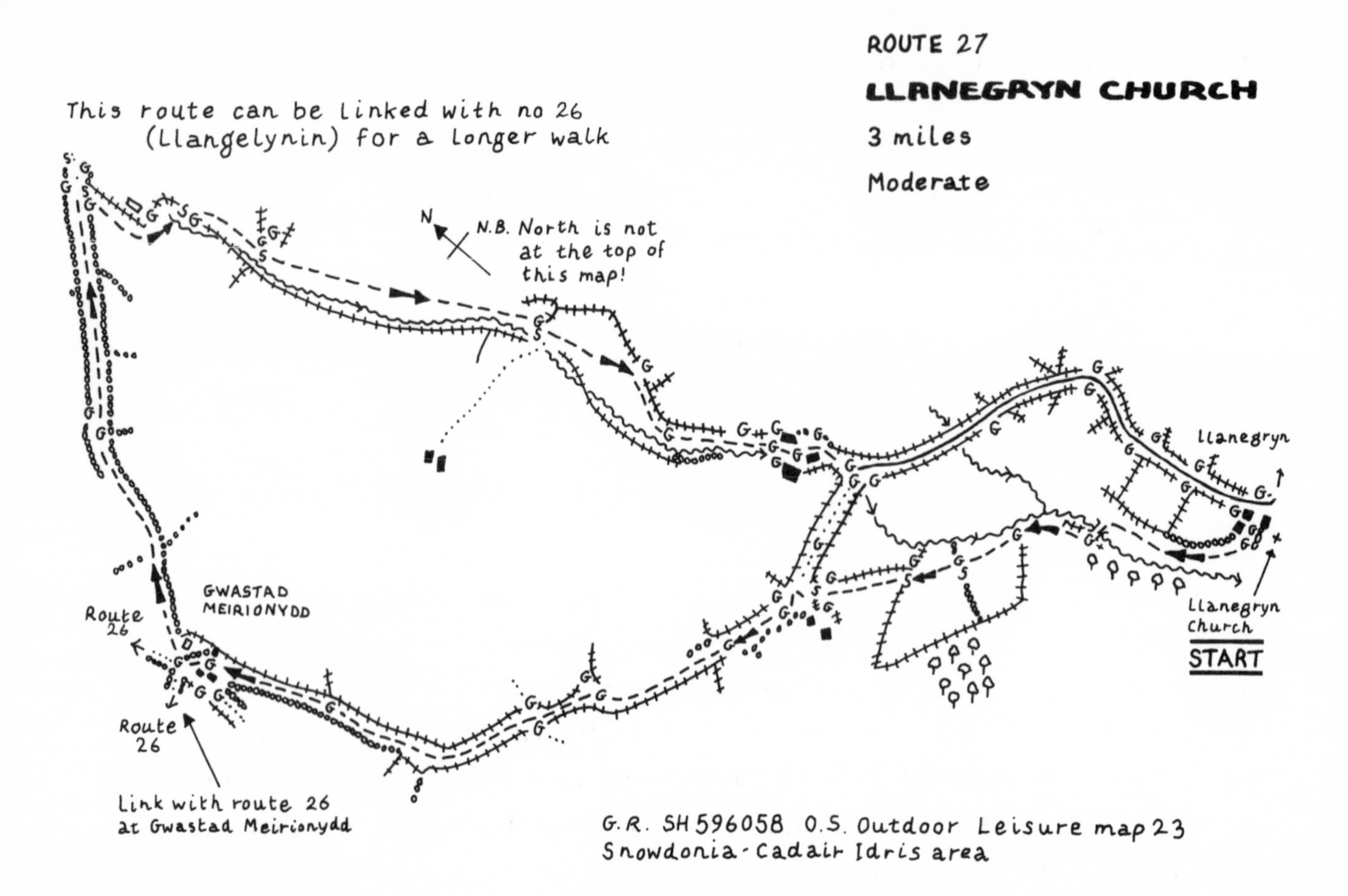

G.R. SH 596058 O.S. Outdoor Leisure map 23
Snowdonia - Cadair Idris area

Route 27 **Llanegryn Church**

<u>**Parking:**</u>
Near Llanegryn church (or at Llangelynin and combine this walk with route 26).

<u>**Public Transport:**</u>
Bus no 28 (Dolgellau-Tywyn) serves Llanegryn (and Llangelynin if this walk is to be combined with route 26).

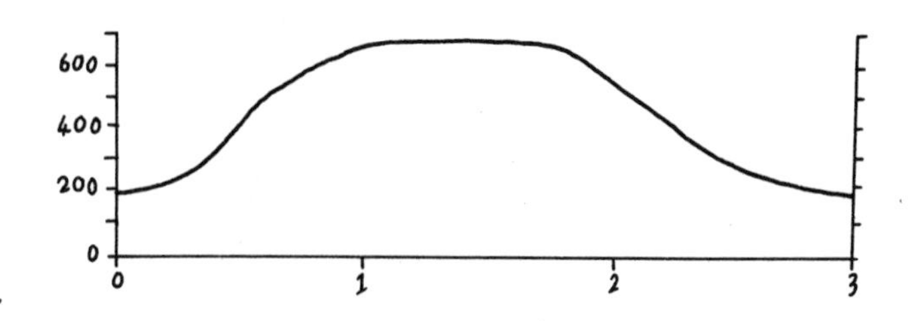

Llanegryn has a very attractive old church which was originally dedicated to St Egryn, its seventh century founder. The present building was built in the 13th century by the Cistercians of Cymer Abbey (see route 14), who dedicated it to St Mary the Virgin. The intricately carved rood loft and screen may have found their way here from Cymer Abbey after the Dissolution. Gwastad Meirionydd is famous for its fairies or 'fairy lights'.

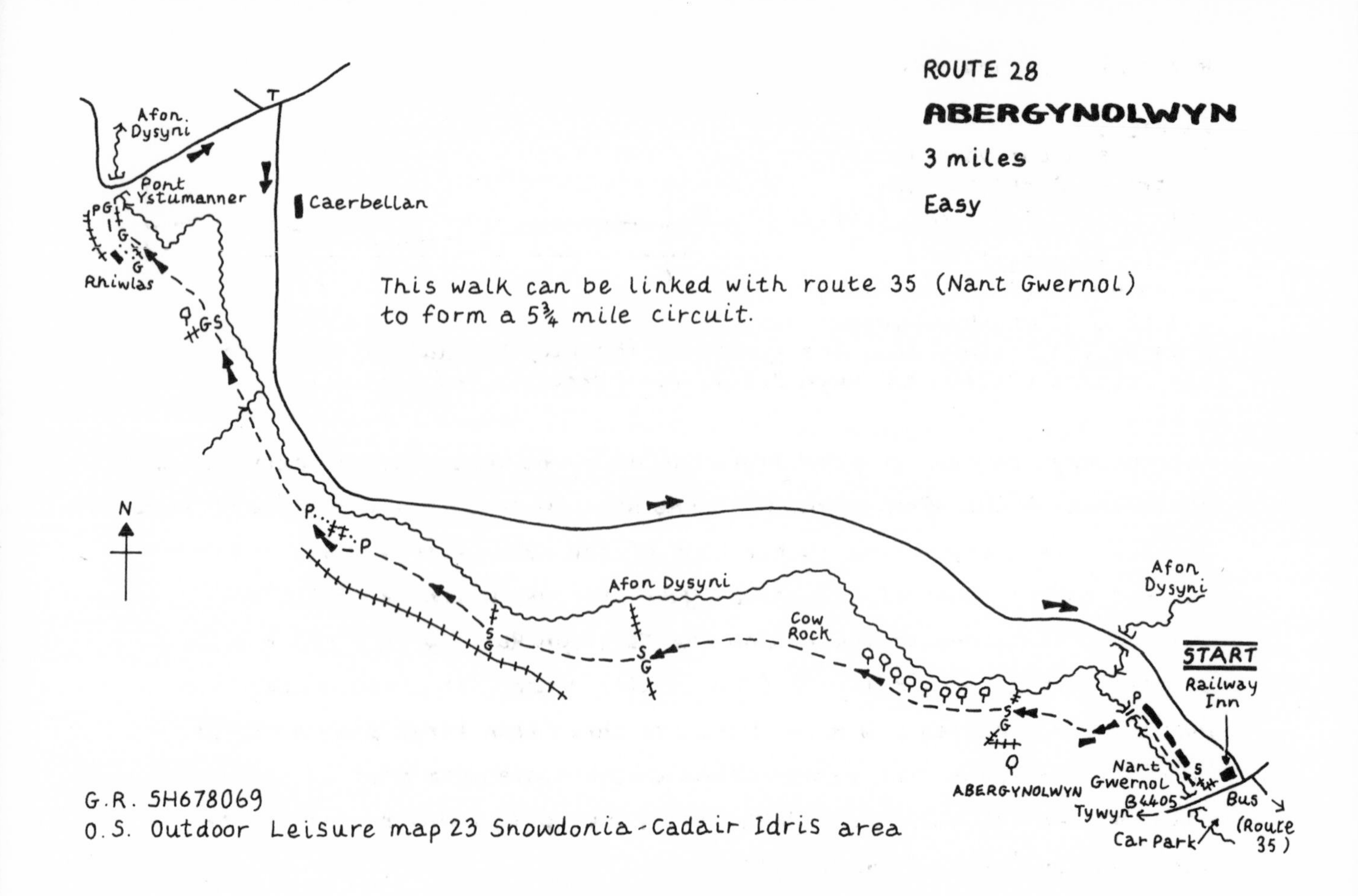
ROUTE 28
ABERGYNOLWYN
3 miles
Easy
This walk can be linked with route 35 (Nant Gwernol) to form a 5¾ mile circuit.
Afon Dysyni
T
Pont Ystumanner
Caerbellan
PG
G
Rhiwlas
GS
N
P
Afon Dysyni
S G
Cow Rock
Afon Dysyni
START
Railway Inn
ABERGYNOLWYN
Nant Gwernol
B4405
Tywyn
Bus
Car Park
(Route 35)
G.R. SH678069
O.S. Outdoor Leisure map 23 Snowdonia-Cadair Idris area

Route 28, **Abergynolwyn**

Parking:
There is a car park in the centre of Abergynolwyn, near Hilary's Kitchen (cafe).

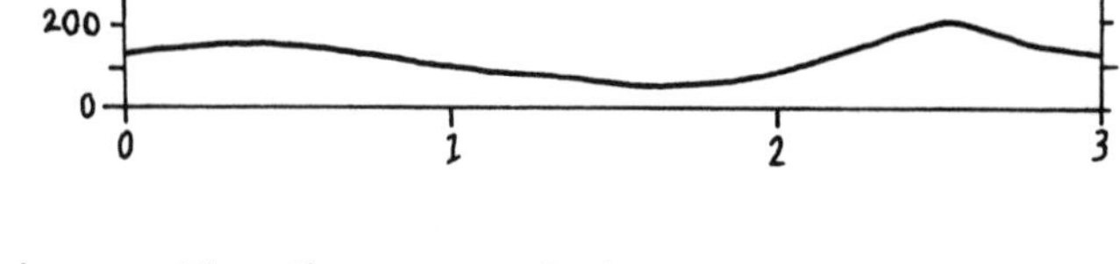

Public Transport:
Buses no 30 (Dolgellau-Tywyn) and 59 (Machynlleth-Tywyn) stop at the Railway Inn, Abergynolwyn. The Talyllyn Railway also serves the village (telephone Tywyn 710472 for timetable information).

Abergynolwyn gained its name from the whirlpool which used to exist at the confluence of the Afon Dysyni with the Nant Gwernol. Its growth came with the slate industry in the latter half of the 19th century. Vast quarries existed to the south of the narrow guage railway which was built to transport the slate to Tywyn. Now the Talyllyn Railway is a major tourist attraction and Abergynolwyn a fine walking centre. This route down the Dysynni Gorge passes Cow Rock. Here are three iron rings plus a trough carved in the rock. The farmer found this a convenient spot to tie up his cows to feed and milk them. Roman coins have been found at Caerbellan - once the home of the Court Jester.

ROUTE 29

TAL-Y-LLYN

2¾ miles

Strenuous

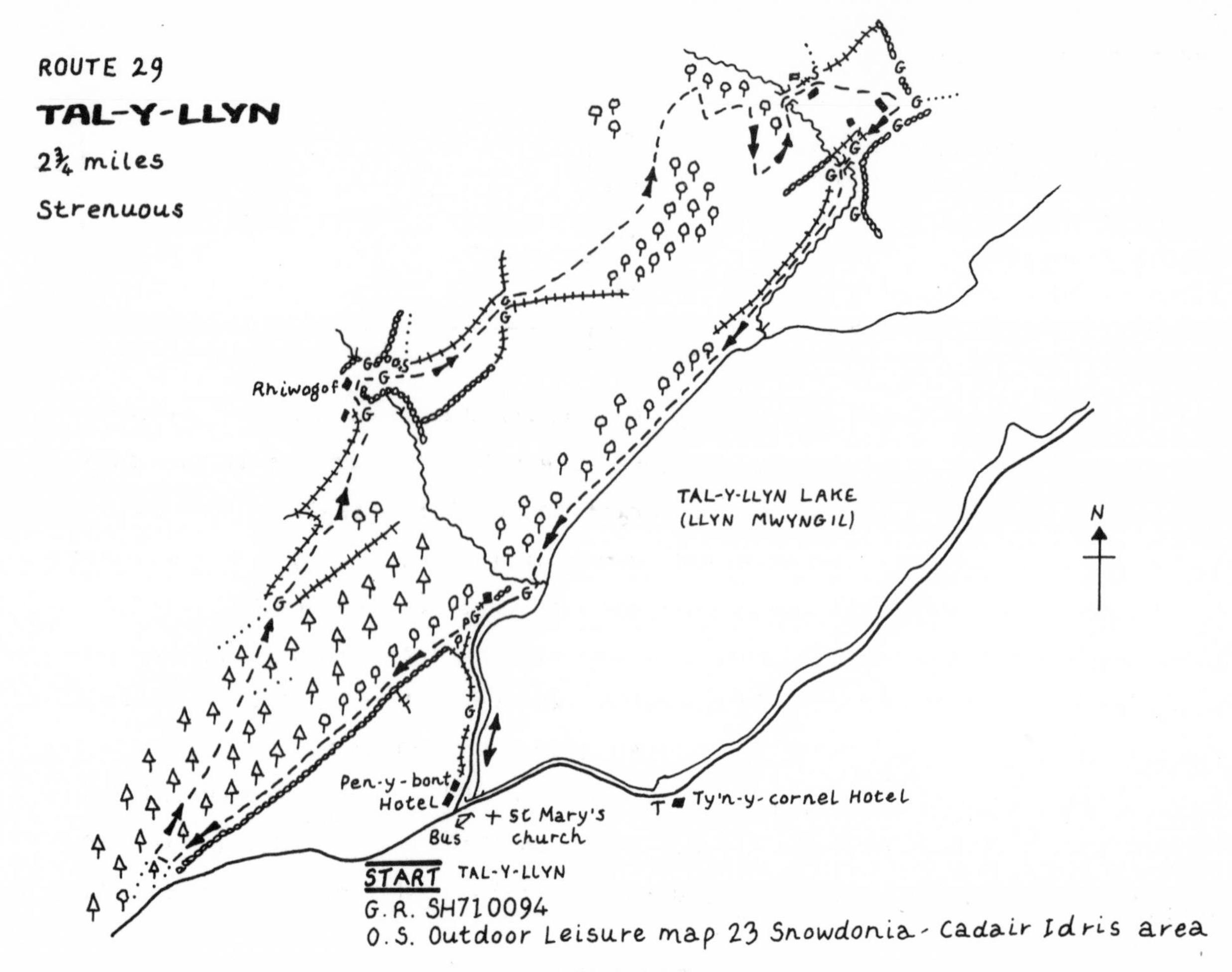

START TAL-Y-LLYN

G.R. SH710094

O.S. Outdoor Leisure map 23 Snowdonia - Cadair Idris area

Route 29, Tal-y-llyn

Parking:
Patrons only can park at the Pen-y-bont Hotel, so become a patron!

Public Transport:
Buses no 30 (Dolgellau-Tywyn) and 59 (Machynlleth-Tywyn) stop at Talyllyn.

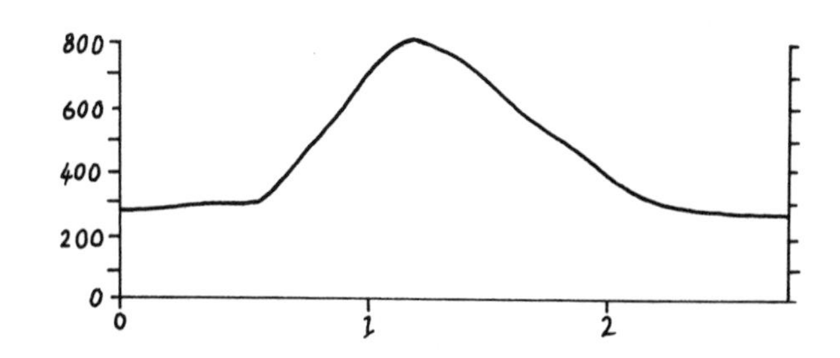

The natural splendour of Tal-y-llyn Lake makes this walk a photographer's paradise. Come on a sunny day and enjoy the reflection of the surrounding mountain slopes in the lake. Don't forget to visit St Mary's church at Talyllyn. Just inside its graveyard, immediately on your right as you enter by the lych gate opposite the Pen-y-bont Hotel, is an ornamental cross marking the grave of Jenny Jones. She was born in Scotland in 1789 and was with her husband of the 23rd Royal Welch Fusiliers at the Battle of Waterloo, remaining on the field three days. They later settled in nearby Corris where her husband was killed in a quarry accident in 1837. Jenny re-married, moved to Talyllyn and died here at the age of 94 on 11th April, 1884. Enter the church to see its arch with painted roses - probably dating from the 15th century.

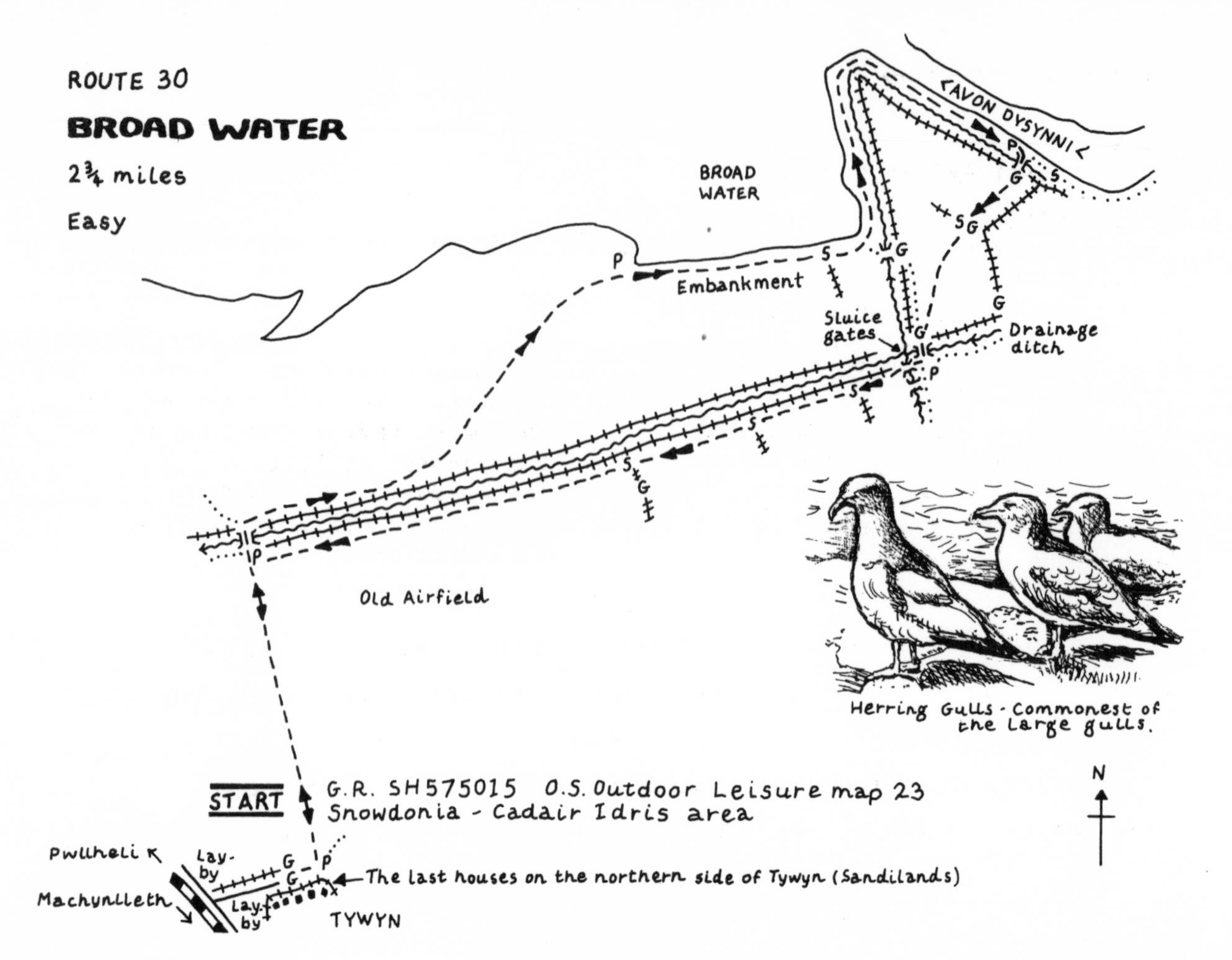

Herring Gulls - Commonest of the large gulls.

Route 30, **Broad Water**

Parking:
There are lay-bys near the start.

Public Transport:
Tywyn is served by British Rail (Machynlleth - Pwllheli Cambrian Coast Line) and by the Talyllyn Railway. There are buses from Dolgellau (no 28 via Fairbourne and no 30 via Talyllyn) and Machynlleth (no 29 via Aberdyfi and no 59 via Corris). Bus no 68 from Tywyn can take you to Sandilands, near the start of this walk.

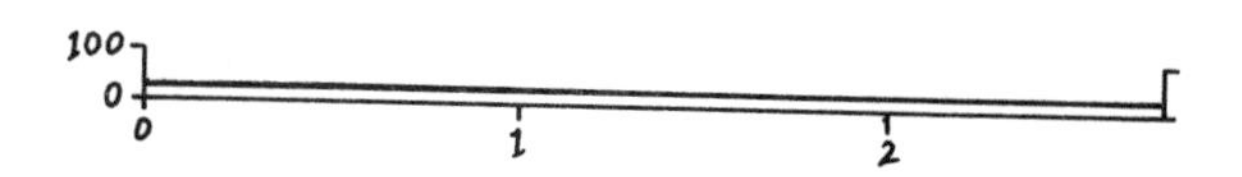

The access road to Sandilands and the start of this walk (after the last of the houses) is Idris Villas. This goes north from Tywyn High Street near the British Rail station.

This is a gentle, dreamy, walk beside the Broad Water which is kept back from Tywyn by an embankment. Look up the beautiful Dysynni Valley for some lovely views. This is an excellent spot for bird-watching, with oystercatcher, redshank, dunlin and other waders to be seen. Wigeon appear in the winter, while mallard, roost, large gull, shelduck and merganser are here all year round.

ROUTE 31

DOMEN DDREINIOG

4 miles

Easy

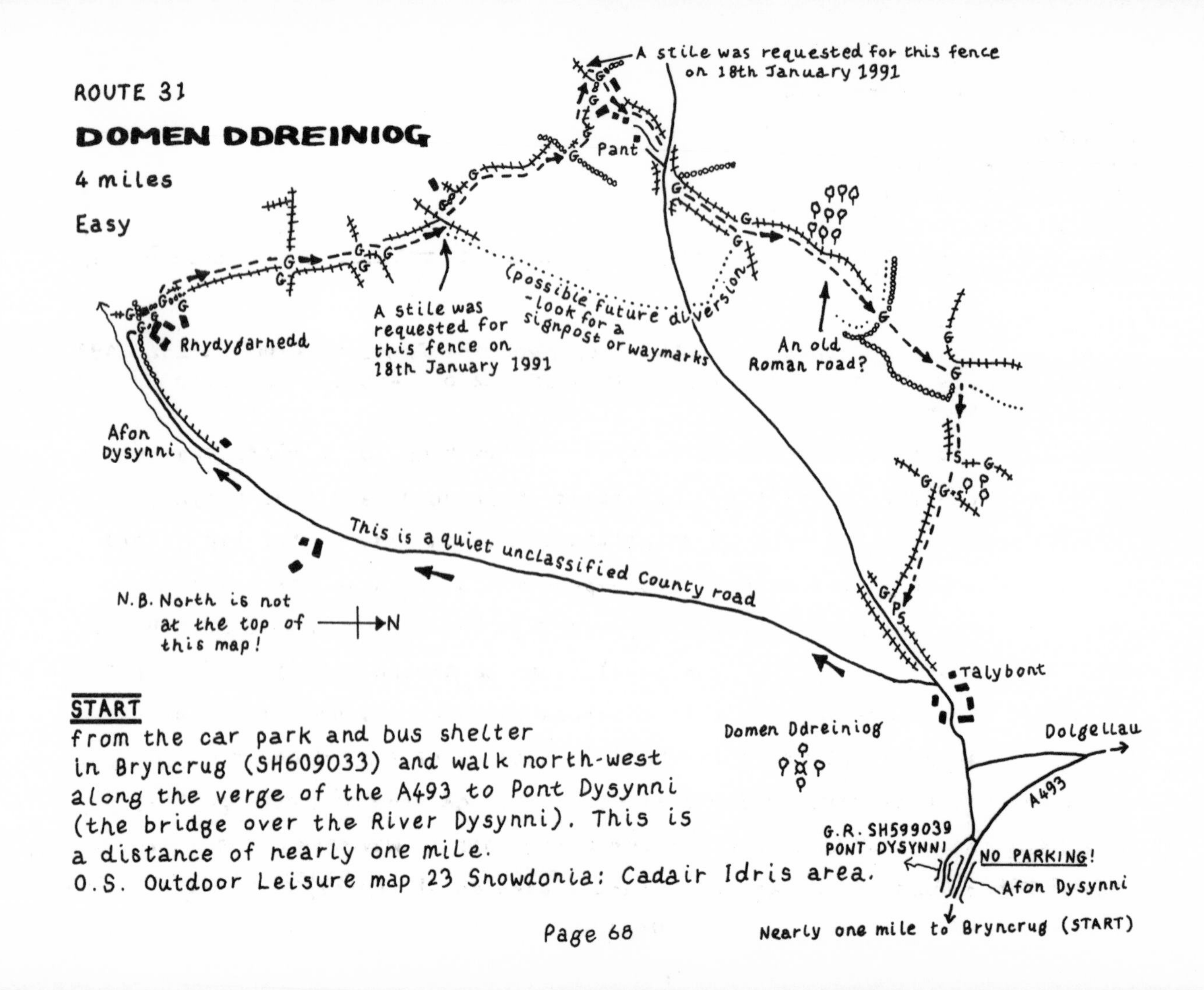

START

from the car park and bus shelter in Bryncrug (SH609033) and walk north-west along the verge of the A493 to Pont Dysynni (the bridge over the River Dysynni). This is a distance of nearly one mile.

O.S. Outdoor Leisure map 23 Snowdonia: Cadair Idris area.

Route 31 Domen Ddreiniog

<u>Parking:</u>

No car parking at Pont Dysynni so park in Bryncrug near the bus shelter (opposite St Matthew's church)

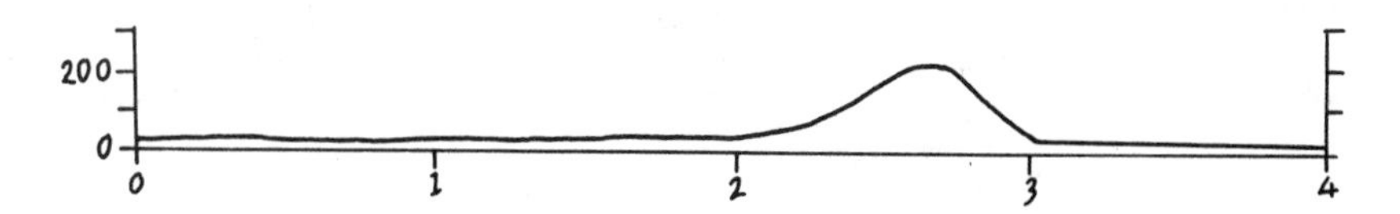

<u>Public Transport:</u>

Buses from Tywyn and Dolgellau (28) stop near the Peniarth Arms on the A493.
Buses from Tywyn and Minffordd (30) stop at the bus shelter opposite St Matthew's church.

There isn't room to show the stretch of road walking (on a wide, grassy verge) between the car park and bus stops in Bryncrug and Pont Dysynni. Simply follow the A493 towards Dolgellau until you come to the big bridge over a wide river. This walk offers superb views, both up the Dysynni Valley towards the distinctive Craig yr Aderyn (Birds' Rock) and over Broad Water. Domen Ddreiniog ('thorny mound') is an earthwork now covered by trees. A medieval fort once guarded a ford across the Afon Dysynni here. Not far away, at Talybont, Llewelyn the Last is said to have held court.

A couple of stiles were needed over fences at the time of writing. They have been requested, but look out for a signpost or waymarks. These may indicate the route of an agreed future diversion of the right of way.

ROUTE 32

NORTH OF RHYDYRONEN STATION

2 miles

Easy

Talyllyn Railway train

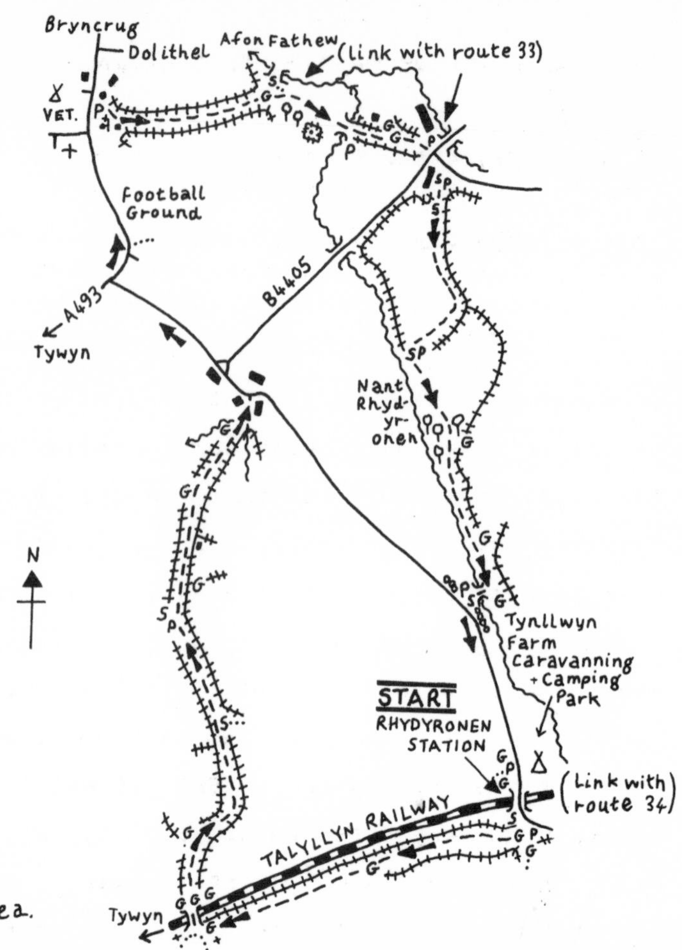

G.R. SH615022 O.S. Outdoor Leisure map 23 Snowdonia: Cadair Idris area.

Route 32, **North of Rhydyronen Station**

Parking:
It would be better to park cars in Bryncrug (see route 33)

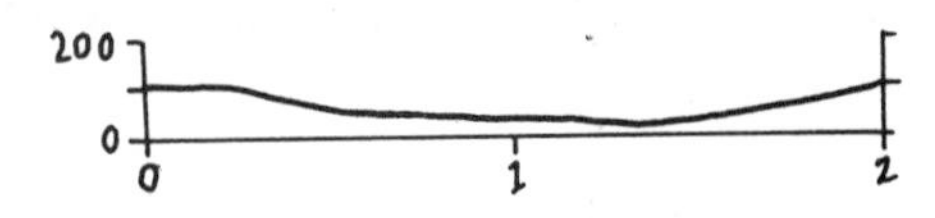

Public Transport:
Come by steam train! The Talyllyn Railway operates a seasonal service from Tywyn and Nant Gwernol. If you come out of season, there are buses to Bryncrug (see route 33).

It would be a sacrilege not to reach the start of this walk by train. If you want value for your fare, combine this route with nos 33 and 34. The Talyllyn Railway was built in the 1860s to carry slate from the quarries above Abergynolwyn to the Cambrian Coast, where Tywyn was already connected to the port of Aberdyfi. The first train ran on the 2ft 3in gauge track through Rhydyronen in 1866. The first passenger services followed in 1867. The line seemed about to shut when Sir Henry Haydn Jones, its owner, died in 1950. He had promised to keep it open during his lifetime, despite the last quarry closing in 1948. It was saved by the formation of the Talyllyn Railway Preservation Society, whose enthusiastic volunteers and a small nucleus of full-time staff help to make a ride on this, the first steam railway to be preserved in this country, a great pleasure.

ROUTE 33

MARY JONES' GRAVE

2½ miles

Easy

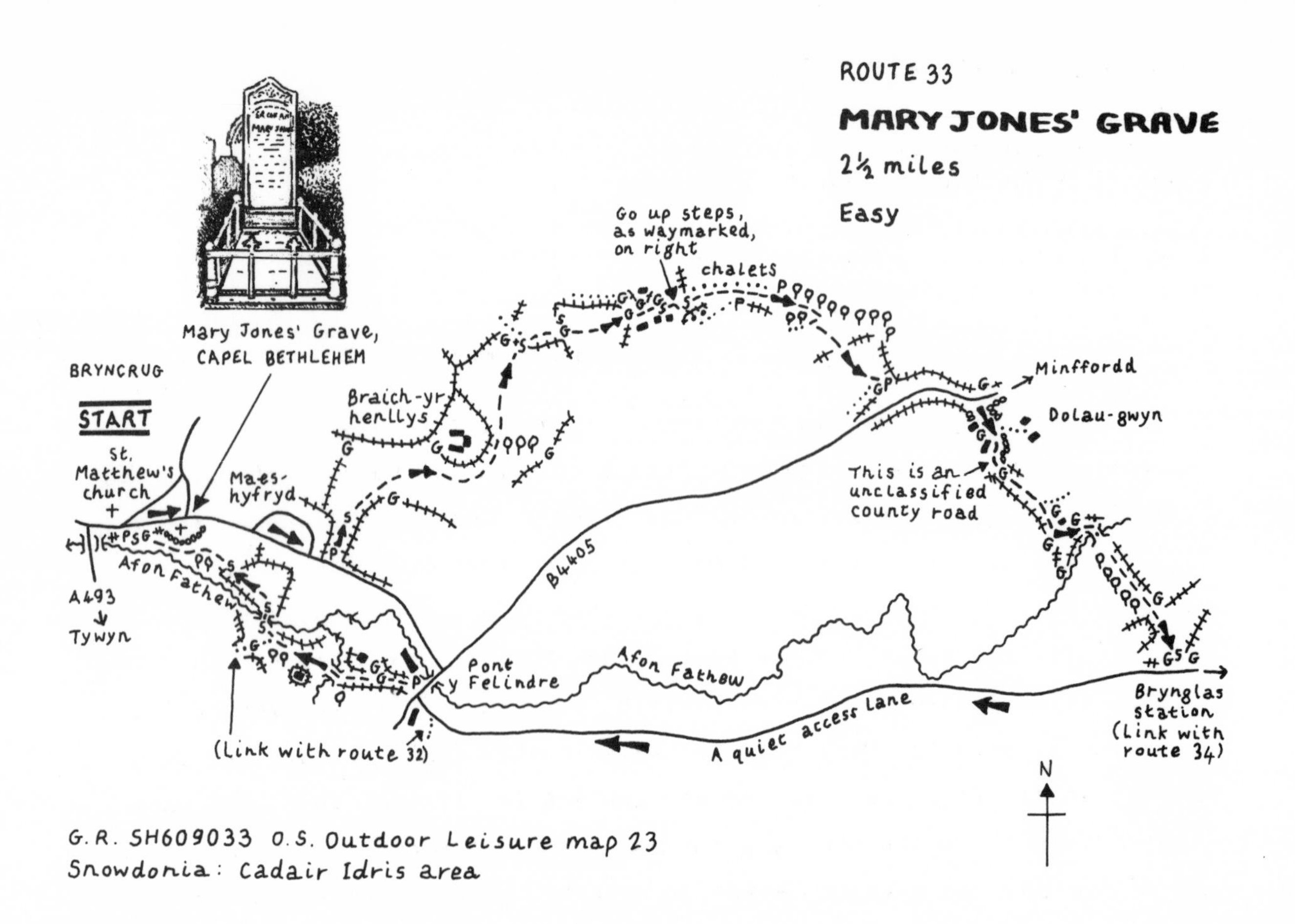

G.R. SH609033 O.S. Outdoor Leisure map 23
Snowdonia: Cadair Idris area

Route 33. **Mary Jones' Grave**

Parking:
Beside the bus shelter and toilets opposite St Matthew's church, Bryncrug.

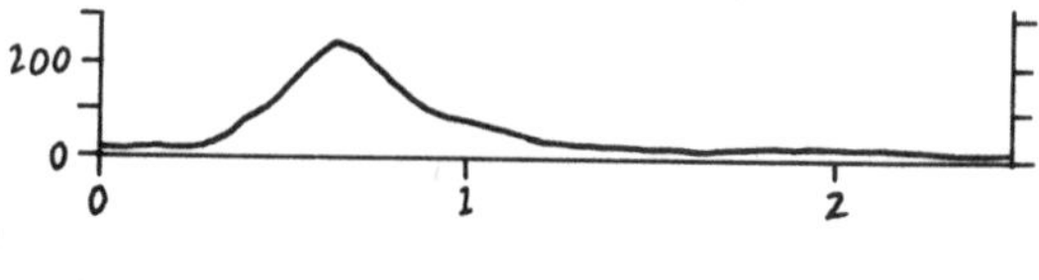

Public Transport:
Buses from Tywyn and Dolgellau (28) stop near the Peniarth Arms on the A493.
Buses from Tywyn and Minffordd (30) stop at the bus shelter opposite St Matthew's church.

Mary Jones achieved fame in 1800 when she made the long trek from her childhood home in Llanfihangel-y-pennant to Bala in the hope of obtaining a copy of the Bible in Welsh. The Rev. Thomas Charles had copies to sell there, but when the 16 year-old Mary arrived after her 30 mile trek, he had sold out. Touched by her story, he gave Mary his own copy and was inspired to help establish the British and Foreign Bible Society in 1804. In 1806 it published the Bible in Welsh, thus satisfying the demand from Welsh Sunday Schools. Mary made her walk in bare feet, to save her only pair of shoes. This route is shorter and easier. It soon takes you past Capel Bethlehem, where Mary was buried in the cemetery in 1864, at the age of 80. She had moved to Bryncrug upon her marriage to Thomas Lewis, a local weaver.

ROUTE 34

BRYNCRUG NUMBER SIX

1½ miles one way (a train ride is recommended for the return, or an extension of this walk by linking it with routes 32 and 33).

Moderate

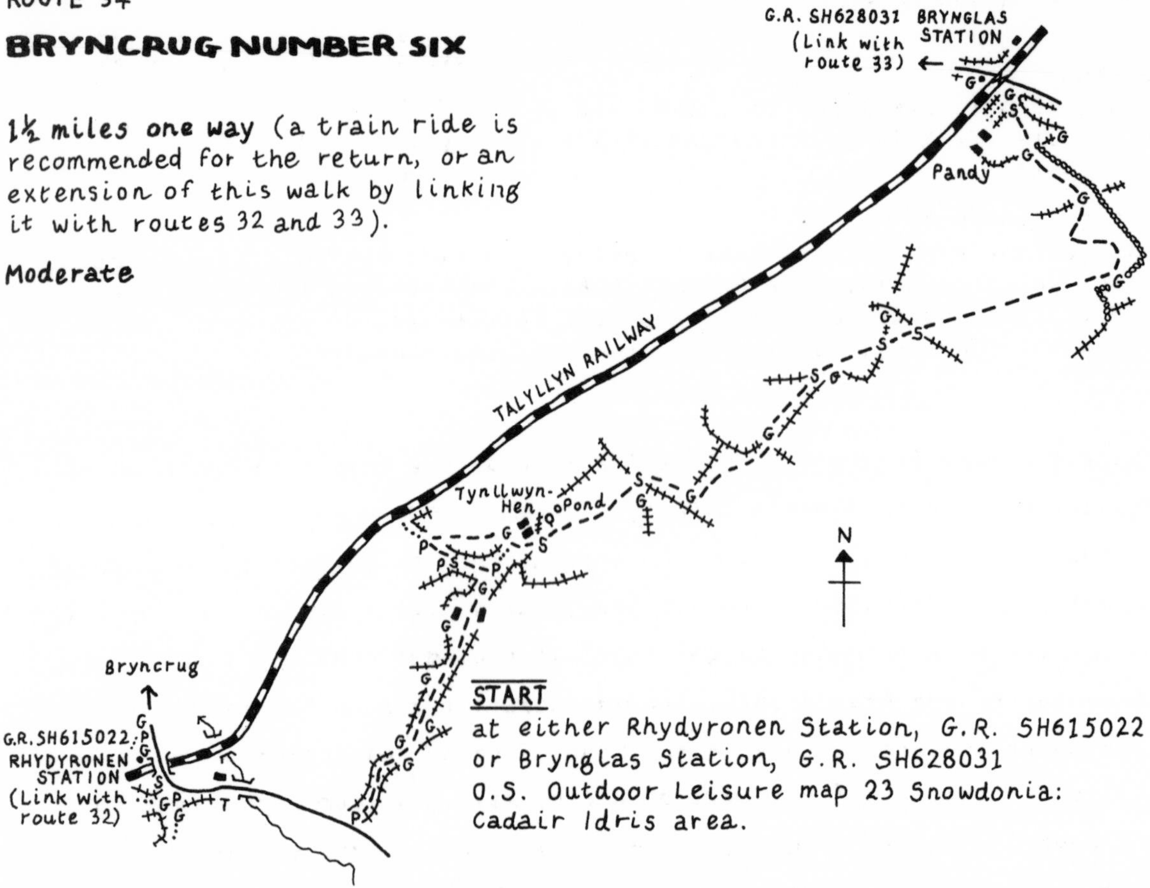

G.R. SH628031 BRYNGLAS STATION
(Link with route 33)
Pandy
TALYLLYN RAILWAY
Tynllwyn-Hen
Pond
N
Bryncrug
G.R. SH615022
RHYDYRONEN STATION
(Link with route 32)

START
at either Rhydyronen Station, G.R. SH615022 or Bryngla s Station, G.R. SH628031
O.S. Outdoor Leisure map 23 Snowdonia: Cadair Idris area.

Route 34, Bryncrug Number Six

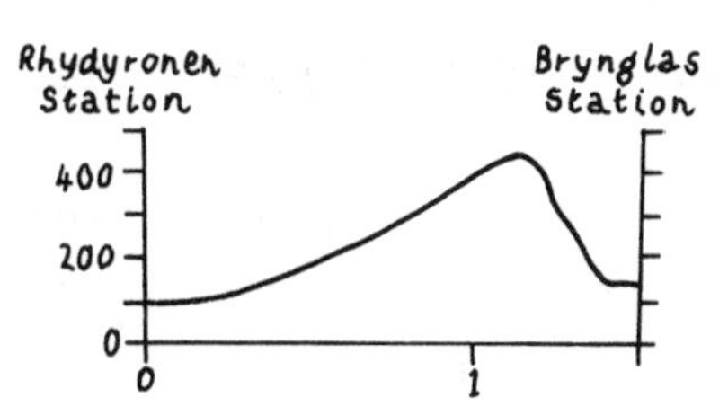

Parking:
Please do not park a car at either end of this route. Park in Bryncrug and link this with route

Public Transport:
Reach either end of this route by enjoying a ride behind a steam engine of the delightful Talyllyn Railway (which runs between Tywyn and Nant Gwernol from Easter to October and over Christmas). If you come out of season there are bus services to Bryncrug (see route 33).

Bryncrug Number Six is the official number of the public footpath which runs between Tynllwyn-Hen and Pandy. It was formerly number 20. When Gwynedd County Council erected six stiles along this route and waymarked it just before Christmas 1990, it opened up a highly attractive path. As you can see when climbing to 437 feet, it provides stunning views across the valley of the Afon Fathew, towards Cadair Idris in the east and over Broad Water to Cardigan Bay in the west. Joining two stations on the Talyllyn Railway, it forms part of a circular walk from Bryncrug when this route is linked with nos 32 and 33. The stiles were erected after a determined campaign by the local group of the Ramblers' Association.

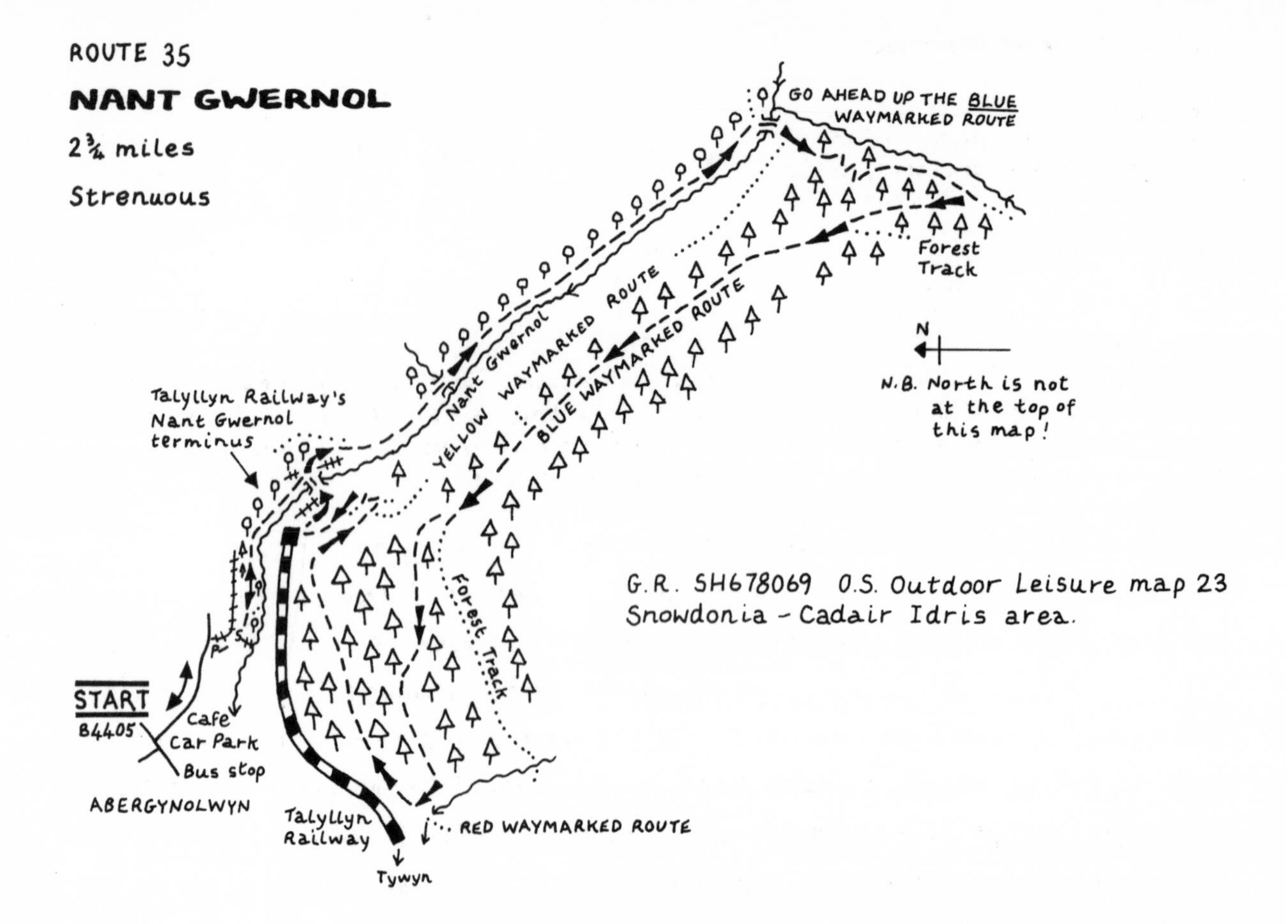
ROUTE 35
NANT GWERNOL
2¾ miles
Strenuous
GO AHEAD UP THE BLUE WAYMARKED ROUTE
Forest Track
Nant Gwernol
YELLOW WAYMARKED ROUTE
BLUE WAYMARKED ROUTE
N
N.B. North is not at the top of this map!
Talyllyn Railway's Nant Gwernol terminus
Forest Track
G.R. SH678069 O.S. Outdoor Leisure map 23 Snowdonia - Cadair Idris area.
START
B4405
Cafe
Car Park
Bus stop
ABERGYNOLWYN
Talyllyn Railway
Tywyn
RED WAYMARKED ROUTE

Route 35, **Nant Gwernol**

Parking:
There is a car park in the centre of Abergynolwyn, near Hilary's Kitchen (cafe).

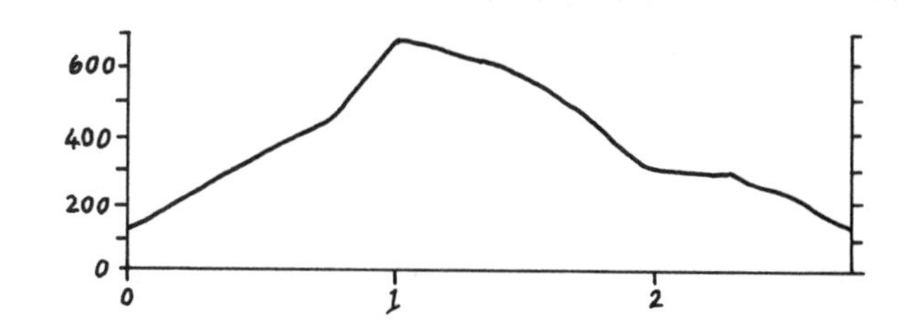

Public Transport:
Buses no 30 (Dolgellau-Tywyn) and 59 (Machynlleth-Tywyn) stop nearby.
Why not make this a truly memorable occasion and come by steam train. Starting and finishing at the Talyllyn Railway's Nant Gwernol terminus would cut half a mile off the walk. Trains run from Tywyn during the tourist season, telephone Tywyn 710472 for details.

Native oak trees provide shade as you start by taking the yellow waymarked route up the valley of the Nant Gwernol (Alder Stream). After crossing a footbridge, go ahead up the blue waymarked route to reach a forest track at nearly 700 feet above sea level. Descend from this through the exotic spruce trees to reach the red waymarked route. Turn away from this to follow the blue route back to the railway terminus. This station was first opened to passengers as recently as 1976. Slate used to fill the trains from here between 1866 and 1947, with passenger services terminating at Abergynolwyn.

ROUTE 36

CWM CADIAN

1½ miles

Moderate

It's always easy to get lost in a forest, so do take care to follow the red waymark posts at first, then ascend at a junction to follow the green waymark posts. A white footprint shows you where to descend from the forest track back to the start, following green waymark posts back down to your outward (red) route.

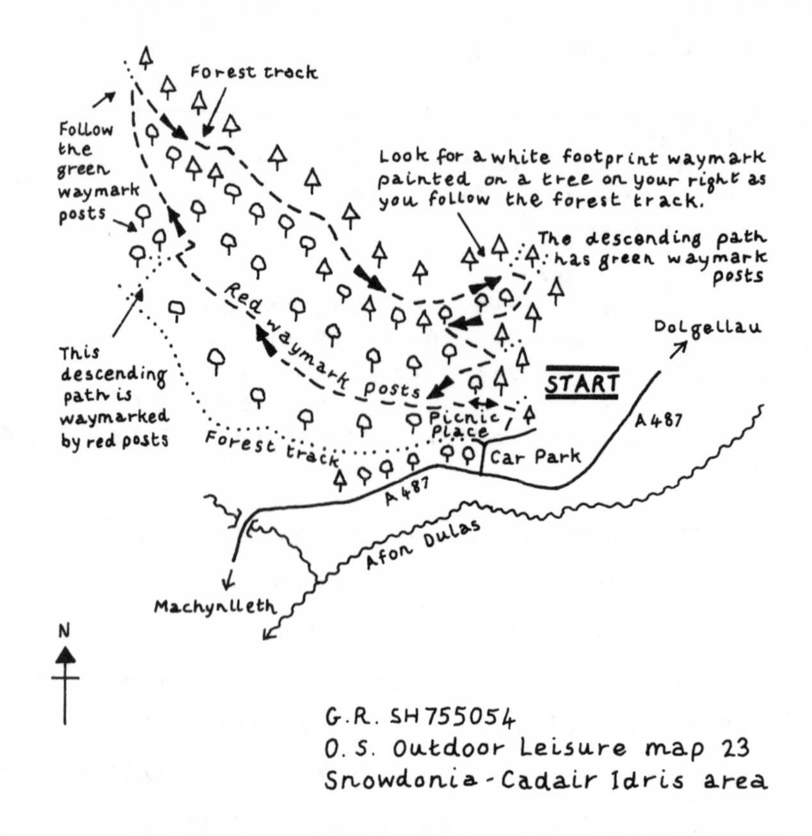

G.R. SH755054

O.S. Outdoor Leisure map 23

Snowdonia - Cadair Idris area

Look out for lorries on the forest track!

Route 36, **Cwm Cadian**

Parking:
There is a car park at the start of this walk, at Tan-y-Coed Picnic Place.

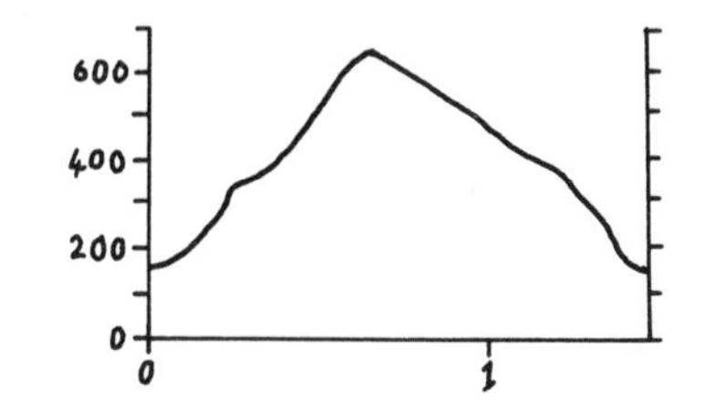

Public Transport:
Buses no 2 (Aberystwyth - Caernarfon), no 34 (Machynlleth - Aberllefenni) and no 59 (Machynlleth - Tywyn via Corris) pass the entrance to the Tan-y-Coed Picnic Place. Ask to be set down here and give vigorous hand signals to be picked up.

The Forestry Commission has waymarked paths through the trees, while a firm forest track is followed at the highest point of this walk. The valley (Cwm Cadian) is named after St Cadfan, who landed at Tywyn in 516 with a party of saints from Brittany (including his cousin St Tydecho of Mawddwy). St Cadfan walked this way often, travelling between his churches at Tywyn and Llangadfan (Montgomeryshire). Happily, not all of the trees here are conifers. Beech trees may shelter woodmice and grey squirrels. The Centre for Alternative Technology is nearby.

KEY TO THE MAPS

Each map is drawn to a scale of six inches to one mile (1:10560) and has a gradient profile showing the height in feet above sea level and the distance in miles from the start of the walk.

SCALE:

0 ONE MILE 1

Symbol	Meaning	Symbol	Meaning
N ↑	Direction of north (n.b. not always at the top of the page)		The footpath route with direction from start
	River or stream with direction of flow		Other paths (not always rights of way)
	Bridge		Motor road
	Wall		Railway
	Hedge or fence		Station or halt
	Trees	P	Signpost
	Buildings	G	Gate
	Ruin	S	Stile
+	Church or chapel		Castle
	Campsite	o	Standing stone

Afon is the Welsh for river, nant means stream